The Teacher's Guide for Supporting Students from Military Families

Ron Avi Astor,
Linda Jacobson, Rami Benbenishty
Hazel R. Atuel, Tamika Gilreath, Marleen Wong,
Kris M. Tunac De Pedro, Monica Christina Esqueda,
and Joey Nuñez Estrada Jr.

TEACHERS COLLEGE PRESS
TEACHERS COLLEGE | COLUMBIA UNIVERSITY
NEW YORK AND LONDON

Military Child Education Coalition®
909 Mountain Lion Circle
Harker Heights, TX 76548

This publication was developed by the USC Building Capacity in Military Connected Schools team, in part, with grant funds from the U.S. Department of Defense Education Activity under Award Number HE1254-10-1-0041. The views expressed in this profile do not necessarily reflect the positions or policies of the Department, and no official endorsement by the Department is intended or should be inferred.

All royalties from the sale of this book are being donated to military children's educational causes.

Published simultaneously by Teachers College Press, 1234 Amsterdam Avenue, New York, NY 10027 and by the Military Child Education Coalition®, 909 Mountain Lion Circle, Harker Heights, Texas 76548

Library of Congress Cataloging-in-Publication Data

The teacher's guide for supporting students from military families / Ron Avi Astor
... [et al.].
   p. cm.
Includes bibliographical references and index.
ISBN 978-0-8077-5369-9 (pbk. : alk. paper)
   1. Children of military personnel–Education–United States. I. Astor, Ron Avi.
LC5081.T43   2012
379.1'21–dc23   2012020712

ISBN 978-0-8077-5369-9 (paperback)

Printed on acid-free paper
Manufactured in the United States of America

19   18   17   16   15   8   7   6   5   4   3

Contents

Preface

As we were writing this book, the war in Iraq officially ended, and a date has been set for withdrawing troops from Afghanistan.

Public support for successful reunions between U.S. service members and their families should be strong, so that our men and women in uniform can make smooth transitions to life back at home. Some parents returning from deployments will be looking for new careers in the face of "downsizing," while others will be training for future assignments overseas. These can be stressful times for military families.

Public schools can potentially provide a setting in which children can feel a sense of security. A "bedrock." "A consistent, safe place." Those are the words one principal we talked to used to describe what school should be for children in military families, "no matter what is going on at home, no matter where you are in the deployment cycle."

We have worked with many military-connected school districts in developing this guide. On a regular basis, we heard stories of how resilient military children are—able to quickly adjust to new schools, new friends, and shifting academic demands. And we've witnessed the love and professionalism in these supportive public schools.

But resiliency isn't necessarily an inborn trait. These fantastic schools are fostering strength, courage, and a sense of pride in these students. They honor and celebrate the many layers of sacrifices made by these families. They are making sure a friendly face is there to greet students when they enroll. They are giving them opportunities to talk about the places they have lived. And they are hiring professionals trained to respond during tough times, so children—many of whom have had to take on adult responsibilities in their homes while a parent is away—can focus on being students.

In searching across the country for good ideas, evidence-supported practices, and grassroots efforts, we've learned that school communities can help to relieve some of the stress on military families. Great schools can help military students and families thrive, provide an extra sense of connectedness, and lend a helping hand when needed.

Schools have generated creative ideas to welcome military children. For example, one school created a friendship garden so military children could literally, and figuratively, put down some roots in their new school and feel more connected.

When another school asked military children to serve as "tour guides" and buddies to incoming students, the transition period went much more smoothly and parents felt less anxious about their children's first days in a new place. And others hosted morning coffee chats for military parents so they could get better acquainted and share ideas for supporting each other.

These are simple practices—but they are practices that can be implemented by any school, and that can create positive experiences for children who move an average of nine times before they graduate from high school.

This book was created by a diverse team of professionals at the University of Southern California. Our research included hours of interviews with military families, model school principals, excellent teachers, and military school liaison officers, as well as observations of programs that are working well. We also carefully integrated research, reviewed the literature, searched the Internet, and explored the work of national organizations in selecting the most beneficial practices, programs, and resources to present.

Our deepest hope is that this book provides you with scientifically sound, practical, and eye-opening ideas for making military families feel more welcome and supported in public schools. We hope civilians will recognize that military culture is an important diversity group to include in curriculum and school climate reform. Ultimately, caring, supportive, culturally appropriate, and thoughtful school environments could radically change the lives of all students, but even more so for those who have endured so much.

All of the royalties from the sale of this book are being donated to nonprofit, education-oriented organizations benefitting military children.

Acknowledgments

This guide seeks to make public schools more supportive of military families. We first want to thank the military families who have sacrificed so much for our country. We thank you for your contributions to our society and to our world. Military families and children are strong, proud, and resilient. We saw and heard this every place we went. Many of the ideas generated in this guide originated from educators who themselves had a military family member or who have served. We thank them for their continued commitment.

The authors wish to sincerely thank the many citizens and professionals in school districts, government, the military, and in nonprofit organizations who have shared their best practices so we could include them in this guide. We especially want to thank the school liaison officers from all branches of the military who work tirelessly to improve school experiences for military children.

To all the district officials, principals, assistant principals, teachers, pupil personnel, parents, and students: thank you for sharing with us your ideas, stories, and photos so that other schools can learn how to make military children feel more welcome and appreciated. Our partners at San Diego State University, UC San Diego, and the University of California Los Angeles have also been instrumental in elevating this work to a regional level. The over 100 master's and doctoral students in social work and education from USC, as well as the master's students in social work, school counseling, and school psychology from SDSU, also deserve special recognition for inspiring many of the recommendations in this book. We thank the undergraduate students in the Partners at Learning program at UCSD.

Many scientific experts and research organizations have advised us through the process of creating this guide, including the members of our International Advisory Board, various educational consultants, the Military Family Research Institute, the National Military Family Association, and the Department of Defense Education Activity (DoDEA).

In particular, we would like to thank: the DoDEA partnership program for national leadership, excellent materials and programs, and vigilant dissemination of best practices to public schools; the Military Child Education Coalition for educating teachers, counselors, parents, and administrators; the American Association of Colleges of Teacher Education for engaging university schools of education; and most importantly, the University of Southern California (USC) schools of social work and education, the Center for Research and Innovation on Veterans and Military Families, and Hamovitch Research Center for their commitment to train professionals in university settings to work with military families. We also want to recognize Dr. Jill Biden, Michelle Obama, and their staffs for support and for nationally prioritizing the needs of military children and families. Their Joining Forces campaign highlights the need to educate universities and public schools about the needs of military students.

Introduction

As a teacher, if I can provide a respite from that stress for the parent left behind and their child, I want to do it. This, in a very small way, is a way for me to give back to my country. Regardless of how I feel about the mission of our military, I support the personnel and their families. After all, the child will benefit educationally from an environment, in school and out, where they feel valued, nurtured, and understood.

—Dale Borgeson, teacher,
Vintage Hills Elementary School, Temecula, California

As a teacher, you typically have little control over the students who come and go through your classroom during the school year. But you can set a tone for your class that is welcoming, caring, and supportive of students' learning and social-emotional development.

This type of environment is especially critical for students from military families, who not only have to change schools often but also face stressful situations unfamiliar to civilian classmates and teachers.

Most students don't relish the thought of having to be the new kid in a school where they don't have any friends, don't know the routines, and might be out of step with the curriculum you are teaching.

There are practices you can use, however, that can help military students feel like valued members of your classroom and contribute to their ongoing success even when they move again.

Accountability systems require you to pay attention to the performance of various groups of students, such as English learners and students with disabilities. If your school serves military students, you should also become informed about how their unique situations affect learning and implement strategies that promote academic achievement and create a sense of community and respect in your classroom.

Children who are born into military families live unique and interesting lives. They have opportunities to travel around the world, to gain firsthand knowledge of cultures that most American students only read about, and can often adapt quickly to new situations and surroundings.

But they also face significant challenges and have special circumstances that civilian children and families don't experience. These can include gaps in school attendance and learning, being separated from a parent who has been deployed, and a sense of isolation in the midst of a civilian community that cannot relate to the obstacles and challenges they face.

In the drive to improve schools, education reformers have focused mainly on the learning needs of minority students, students with disabilities, English learners, and even preschool-age children. But they have rarely considered the academic and social needs of one particular group—students from military families.

In your preservice preparation, you probably were not trained to recognize the unique circumstances and challenges that children face when they grow up in a military family, and schools, by and large, have not created environments in which military children feel welcomed and supported.

One explanation for this gap in knowledge and practice could be that many educators and even policymakers have the misconception that all service members' children live on bases and attend Department of Defense Education Activity (DoDEA) schools. In fact, even many education researchers tend to make generalizations about military children based on findings that pertain only to students who attend schools and preschools operated by the DoDEA.

In reality, only about 7% of U.S. military children—about 86,000—attend schools and preschools operated by DoDEA. These schools—located both in the States and on bases overseas—have staff that are trained and prepared to respond to the needs of military children and families. But the *vast majority* of military children attend regular public schools with staff that may or may not be familiar with or sensitive to the realities of military life, such as frequent moves and the deployment of a parent. They are "military-connected schools," according to the government's definition, because at least 3% of their students have parents in the military, but their understanding of military culture and their ability to address related challenges varies significantly.

In addition, there are more than a million students whose parents are serving in the National Guard and Reserves. These students live typical civilian lives, but when their parents' units are called into action, they are suddenly thrust into an unfamiliar military lifestyle. These students may also require special attention and understanding in their public school. Research finds that their parents are less likely to have access to or use support services offered by the military.

It might also be helpful for you to realize that, because military members are often young, sometimes you may have a student who has an older brother or sister that is deployed. Moreover, because of the heavy involvement of the Guard and Reserves in Iraq and Afghanistan, some children have grandparents that have been deployed.

Because of these factors, military students in your school may feel misunderstood, and you may feel in the dark about how to best support them in the classroom. There are, however, some districts and schools that are doing a remarkable job working with military families. The practices and programs they have implemented need to be shared with broader audiences so that all schools serving military children are better equipped to include these families as part of the school community and respond to their concerns.

Teachers like you can make a significant impact not only on a child's academic success, but also on their social and emotional well-being. If your school serves military students, it is critical that you become more aware of this group and acquire strategies to support them. Organizations such as the Military Child Education Coalition, for example, have created popular workshops and materials focused on education issues related to military families. There are very few evidence-based programs, however, aimed at creating a more military-friendly culture in civilian schools.

DESCRIPTION OF THIS GUIDE

The goal of this resource guide is to provide a toolkit of ideas and promising practices that have been generated by educators working within military-connected schools. Part of a 4-year project called "Building Capacity to Create Highly Supportive Military-Connected School Districts," this guide is a groundbreaking effort to bring educators into the conversation about how to make schools more inviting and supportive for this unique group of students. The project, supported in part by a grant from DoDEA to a consortium of eight school districts and the University of Southern California, is focused on improving school climate so that the education community is more welcoming to military children. Our goal is to give educators strategies to support these students' academic progress and social and emotional well-being, and to encourage all school staff members to recognize the sacrifices that military children make because of their parents' service.

In addition to this guide, we have also written companion versions for pupil personnel, school administrators, and military parents. You can inform people in those roles about the guides that are appropriate for them.

The lives of military children are receiving attention at the highest levels of government. A 2011 presidential initiative boosted efforts across all federal agencies to support military families—a focus that is expected to continue in future administrations.

In addition, the Department of Defense and the Department of Education have agreed that supporting military children in civilian schools should be a high priority, and that traditional public and private schools and

DoDEA schools should begin sharing information about successful practices and policies.

This guide will:

- highlight many of those practices and strategies that you can use to make your classroom more welcoming for military families and support students' academic and social-emotional needs.
- inform you about many of the recurring issues military students may face, such as school mobility, family stress created by a parent's deployment or return home, and exposure to trauma.
- refer you to organizations and services you can use as resources to learn more about the concerns of military children and families. *Special Note: We have listed website links for all of the resources that we have included, but do realize that links change or disappear. Search online for the organizations or names of articles if a link no longer works.*
- draw attention to needs and opportunities for further research.

THE ISSUE OF TRANSITION

When a child grows up with one or both parents in the armed services, it's inevitable that he or she will change schools much more often than nonmilitary students. But the life of a military child is an ongoing series of transitions that take place even when a physical relocation is not involved. This is important to keep in mind, so transition is a theme that will cut across all topics addressed in this guide.

Every time a parent is deployed or returns from an assignment ("reintegration") is a transition that can lead to changing roles in the family structure and routine or changing relationships with parents.

Simply being "the new kid" in school is not the only time a military child may become distracted by the shifting nature of his or her home environment. Making new students feel welcome is one responsibility that schools have, but it is also important to provide ongoing support for military students in the school setting.

"[Children] need something that they can rely on that's consistent, especially with multiple deployments," says Diana Ashe, a mother, a former Marine, and the wife of a Marine. She also holds a Master's of Social Work from USC. "The more constant structure you can have within a school and everybody working within a community and as a group, the better off the kids will be."

It is our hope that this guide gives you the knowledge and resources you need to create a supportive classroom for military children.

CHAPTER 1

An Introduction to Military Culture

To best serve the military children and families in your classroom, it's useful to first understand their unique lifestyle. Currently, less than 1% of the population serves in the military. As a result many members of civilian society are unfamiliar with military culture. Military culture, much like any culture, "is comprised of values, beliefs, traditions, and norms that govern the social behavior of service members," write Herbert Exum, Jose Coll, and Eugenia Weiss in their 2011 book *A Civilian Primer for Counseling Military Veterans* (p. 17).

These authors, having many years of service in the military and working with military families, say that such values, beliefs, traditions, and norms determine how members of the military and veterans conduct themselves from "the moment they enter military status" (p. 19). Though values may differ, to a degree, by branch, "honor, courage, loyalty, integrity, and commitment" are held in high esteem across all military branches (p. 17).

Even as you read this chapter, however, remember not to make generalizations about military students. Even though military families share cultural characteristics due to their military affiliation, each family has other characteristics—ethnicity, socioeconomic status, past experiences in public schools, etc.—that also shape their opinions and actions.

CODES OF CONDUCT

Just as norms and laws dictate behavior within civilian societies and cultures, standards of conduct govern how service members think and act, write Exum and colleagues. Remaining committed to these standards is considered critical to the mission and success of the armed forces. Following the chain of command is among the most significant codes of conduct. In their book, Exum and colleagues cite World War II veteran Willard Waller, who in 1944 wrote:

> chain of command refers to the succession of commanding officers from superior to subordinate through which command is exercised via orders. [The chain of

command] settles all questions of authority and avoids clashes of personality through a hierarchal system in which everyone has a place in relation to the other. Orders come from the top down and never from the bottom up. Everyone is under orders and there can never be any doubt regarding who has the right to order whom to do what (p. 21).

Continuing on the topic, Exum and colleagues write that the hierarchal nature of the chain of command ensures that

social status in the military is very clear, whereby officers have higher status than enlisted personnel and both officers and enlisted personnel are further ordered in status according to rank. Duties, responsibilities, pay, living arrangements and social interactions are all determined by rank, and appropriate insignia displayed on the military uniform easily identifies rank. Superiors and subordinates are clearly delineated, and one's place in the social structure is never ambiguous (p. 24).

As a teacher, you might find that military parents expect your school (and perhaps your parent organization) to function in the same way. They might not be open to advice or direction from a teacher or counselor and may instead demand the principal's approval of any decision involving their children. Furthermore, they may expect administrators to "discipline" staff, similar to the way issues are handled by the military command.

MILITARY FAMILIES

Of the 2.2 million individuals serving in active, National Guard, or Reserve units in 2009, approximately 55% were married and 40% had at least two children, notes Major Eric Flake, a physician at Madigan Army Medical Center. The number of dual-career couples in which both parents are serving active duty is also increasing, historian Anni Baker noted in 2008.

These families—including the children—share a unique cultural context. Similar to their loved ones serving in uniform, military culture exerts "normative pressures on the behavior of [military children and their families]. Family members informally carry the rank of the servicemembers, and behavioral prescriptions vary accordingly," wrote University of Maryland sociologist Mady W. Segal in a 1989 article, "The Nature of Work and Family Linkages: A Theoretical Perspective" (pp. 23–24). Baker emphasized that "on or off base, there is great pressure to conform to common standards of behavior." And, according to Segal, failure to do so may negatively impact their loved one's career goals.

SEEKING HELP

Within the military, problems are addressed according to the chain of command. Depending on the severity of the issue and how it might be perceived, a service member may be hesitant to report or seek help for individual problems. Service members may be reluctant to report individual health problems, especially mental health issues. Military culture has traditionally viewed mental illness as a sign of weakness, but this is a perception that the military is working to change. Nevertheless, signs of psychological illness may result in the service member being "perceived as unfit for duty" or worse yet, a security risk, thus limiting opportunities for career advancement, Exum and colleagues write. For these reasons, service members may sometimes not seek help.

This characteristic may also affect how the family interacts with you and other staff members at your school. Mindful that their behavior is subject to scrutiny and may negatively impact their loved one's career, members of military families may be reluctant to seek help. Therefore, military children who are struggling academically and/or emotionally may not be able to access necessary supports. Asking for help would draw unwanted attention to the family and service member.

Military family members may also worry that their child's problem will be perceived as a sign of weakness, Segal noted. To effectively support military families and children in need, you should first understand the unique cultural contexts of military families. Military parents may be resistant to interventions that target specific children since this approach would contradict the military's emphasis on groups over individuals. Support services and interventions may be more effective if delivered within a group setting. Any offer to help the child should be accompanied by respect and information. Supports must also *empower* military families, psychology professor Charles Figley, now at Tulane University, wrote in his 1993 chapter, "Weathering the Storm at Home: War-Related Family Stress and Coping."

WHEN WORLDS COLLIDE: CONTRASTING MILITARY AND CIVILIAN CULTURES

In addition to different attitudes toward seeking help, there are other ways in which the military families in your school may differ from nonmilitary families. Individuals who serve in the military form a distinct cultural group. Unlike U.S. civilian culture, which emphasizes individuality and personal freedom, military culture imposes "a strict hierarchal structure" that is "mission" focused, Exum and colleagues write (p. 24). Following the chain of command, obeying orders, and group solidarity are critical to fulfilling the mission. Given the pervasive nature of military culture, service members may be less comfortable interacting with civilians who are unfamiliar with military culture. The majority of service members, however, "are compelled to live in" civilian residential communities for a significant proportion of their career, Roger W. Little wrote in the 1971 *Handbook of Military Institutions.*

Therefore, service members and their families spend a substantial amount of time surrounded by civilian culture. The service member's interactions and participation in civilian culture, however, require adaptation that extends beyond simply removing one's uniform. Service members must navigate the norms, cultural codes, and social behaviors of civilians, such as public school staff. Tensions may therefore arise if the service member, or civilian, is unable to reconcile cultural differences, Exum and his co-authors write.

BENEFITS OF MILITARY SERVICE

While a number of demands are placed on military families, there are also a number of advantages that accompany military life. Lindsay Paden and Laurence Pezor emphasized this aspect in their 1993 article, "Uniforms and Youth: The Military Child and His or Her Family." "The opportunity to travel, to see different parts of the world and [to engage with] a variety of cultures," is unique, they write (p. 11). And instead of leading to problems, adversity in military families can provide opportunities for children to mature. Finally, given their collective circumstances, military families share an identity and bond that has endured over time, write Paden and Pezor.

It's clear that military culture is fundamentally different from civilian culture. Recognizing this fact and making an effort to understand military families' values, beliefs, traditions, and social norms can help schools better serve military children.

GLOSSARY OF TERMS

The education field is filled with jargon, acronyms, and terms that non-educators in your school may not understand. Likewise, the military has its own "language" that civilians may not know other than what they have heard on television or in the movies. Becoming familiar with many of these terms can help you become more informed about the military families in your school.

Active Duty: continuous duty on a daily basis; comparable to the civilian term "full-time employment."

Promising Practice Spotlight

The birth of the U.S. Marine Corps is celebrated each year with a cake-cutting ceremony in which the first slice is given to the oldest Marine present, who then hands it to the youngest Marine. The ritual represents the passing of knowledge and experience from older Marines to the next generation.

Students at Jefferson Middle School, located on the Camp Pendleton Marine Corps Base, shared in that tradition when the Marine Corps celebrated its 235th birthday on November 10, 2010. The ceremony illustrates what schools serving military students can do to integrate a military-themed ritual into the school day and make it relevant for all students.

Kim Becker, then a student in the USC School of Social Work—who specializes in military social work and was completing her internship at Jefferson—organized the event as an effort to recognize students at the school whose parents serve in the Marines. The ceremony was also intended to create more awareness among nonmilitary students.

"I wanted to allow all children to be exposed to the military culture, cause, and traditions," Becker, a Marine wife, told the *San Diego Union-Tribune*. "I also wanted to help military students here feel a sense of belonging, and create community cohesion between the base and the school."

Chris Hurst, the school's principal and a former Marine, used the event as an opportunity to encourage students to pursue excellence both in and out of school.

"Military children were acknowledged for their resiliency and culture," Becker wrote in her summary of the event, adding that she "hopes to see this project replicated within all military-impacted schools as a way to educate students and teachers about the military culture and lifestyle."

Schools serving students whose parents are in other branches of the military might want to find out which ceremonies would be appropriate to replicate in those communities.

Typical Marine birthday cake

BAH: Basic Allowance for Housing. Monthly housing assistance provided to service members who live off the military installation or in private housing on the installation.

Battalion: a unit of 300–1,000 soldiers under the command of a lieutenant colonel.

Brigade: a unit of 3,000–5,000 soldiers under the command of a colonel.

Care Package: a package sent from home containing food and/or personal items.

Chain of Command: the succession of commanding officers from a superior to a subordinate through which commands are executed; also the organizational structure of a branch of the armed forces: squad, platoon, company, battalion, brigade, division, corps, and army.

CO: Commanding Officer.

Company: a unit of 62–190 soldiers led by a captain.

Corps: the Marine Corps; also a unit of 20,000–40,000 soldiers under the command of a lieutenant general.

DoDDS: Department of Defense Dependent Schools. Schools operated in the United States and overseas by the Department of Defense Education Activity (DoDEA).

Dependent: a family member for whom a service member is legally and financially responsible—usually a spouse or child.

Deploy: to systematically station military persons or forces over an area; also the movement of forces within an area of military operation; the positioning of forces in a formation for battle. The term refers to military personnel being on temporary assignment away from their home base over an extended period of time.

Division: a unit of 10,000–15,000 soldiers under the command of a major general.

Inactive Reserve: affiliation with the military in a non-training, non-paying status after completing the minimum obligation of active duty service.

IED: Improvised Explosive Device.

Lifer: career military personnel.

MEPS: Military Entrance Processing Station. Military bases at various locations in the United States that receive and train new enlisted personnel.

MIA: Missing In Action.

MOS: Military Occupational Specialty.

NCO: Non-Commissioned Officer; an enlisted person ranked sergeant (E-4) or above.

Obligation: the period of time an individual agrees to serve on active duty, in the Reserves, or a combination of both.

OCS: Officer Candidate School. A program for college graduates with no prior military training that wish to become military officers. The program also accepts qualified enlisted personnel who wish to become officers.

Rank: Grade or official standing of commissioned and warrant officers.

Reserves: the military forces comprised of individuals who are not presently on full-time active duty but who may be called to active duty if needed.

R&R: rest and relaxation.

Sea Duty: an assignment (generally for 3 years) to any ship, whether or not scheduled for deployment, or to any aircraft squadron that may or may not be deployable; the term typically refers to Navy personnel.

Stand Down: a 3-day rest period for units coming out of the field.

Tour of Duty: a specified period of service obligation; also used to describe the location of a duty tour.

Sources: "Students at the Center," DoDEA (http://www.militaryk12partners. dodea.edu/studentsAtTheCenter/index.html); Exum et al., (2011)

FACTS AND FIGURES

Total Force Demographics (as of March 2011)

- Approximately 203,800 individuals are currently deployed (including Reservists and Guardsmen)
- Approximately 35% of the deployed force in Iraq and Afghanistan was comprised of Guardsmen and Reservists
- Approximately 200,000 women serve in the military

Casualties and Wounded (as of July 2011)

- Operation Iraqi Freedom (3/19/03–8/31/10): 4,421 casualties; 31,922 wounded
- Operation New Dawn (began 9/1/01): 56 casualties; 224 wounded
- Operation Enduring Freedom (began 10/7/01): 1,647 casualties; 12,450 wounded
- Traumatic Brain Injuries: 212,742 (total since 2000, as of March 2011)

Sources:

- Coll, J., Hassan, A., Rank, M., Reyes, V. A., & Wildy, M. (2011). Military culture [PowerPoint presentation]. University of Southern California.
- Defense and Veterans Brain Injury Center. (2011). *Traumatic brain injury: Numbers.* Available at http://dvbic.org/TBI-Numbers.aspx
- U.S. Department of Defense. (2011). *Military personnel statistics.* Available at http://siadapp.dmdc.osd.mil/personnel/MILITARY/miltop.htm
- U.S. Department of Defense. (2011). *News: Casualty status.* Available at http://www/defense.gov/news/

CHAPTER 2

Mobility

Changing schools frequently can have negative effects on students and their academic performance. Highly mobile students can fall behind in school because of missing days during a move or because of problems adjusting to new schools, classmates, and teachers.

Changing schools can contribute to children feeling sad, depressed, or angry, which can be displayed in a variety of ways in your classroom, including poor behavior. Research findings on the social-emotional outcomes of frequent school transfers, however, are less conclusive than those on academic effects. Some children seem to grow more resilient with each move.

MOBILITY AND MILITARY CHILDREN

For children in military families, these mobility issues are compounded. They move three times more often than those in civilian families, and as a result can experience academic setbacks and other problems in schools. In addition, the school moves that military children experience may make the normal transitions that students encounter—such as the move from elementary to middle school or middle to high school—more troublesome than they would be for students who haven't experienced so many changes.

Research suggests, however, that the military lifestyle doesn't have to hinder students' chances of staying on top of their schoolwork or make them

Key Points on Student Mobility

- Frequent school moves can cause students to fall behind academically and develop social/emotional problems.
- Mobility, however, doesn't affect every child the same way.
- Research provides insight into how mobility affects children in military families.
- Teachers can use strategies in their classrooms to ease the stress and difficulty for students that come with changing schools. These practices don't have to require policy changes, additional funding, or special training.

Major Challenges for Military Students When They Change Schools

- Academic Standards
- Extracurricular Activities
- Special Education
- Parental Involvement
- Social Adjustment

feel like outcasts in a new school. Some students may react positively to the experience because they get a chance to start over.

Be aware that military families sometimes think their service to the country is not being recognized or appreciated when they encounter policies or rules that seem to disregard the unique circumstances of military children. Your classroom, however, can and should also be part of a support network that assists students in making transitions between schools. There are strategies that you can use to make new students feel welcome and in step with the rest of the class.

In general, experts say that more research is needed on what classroom teachers can do to effectively teach and welcome military or other highly mobile students. Leslie Grant and colleagues from the College of William and Mary observed teachers who had received awards for being highly successful with at-risk students (Grant, Stronge, & Popp, 2008). They recommended that state and national organizations begin recognizing and honoring teachers who work with highly mobile students.

Education research often cannot be generalized to the military student population. The knowledge that exists on student mobility tends to be based on other highly mobile groups, such as homeless students or children in foster care. While military children may have some needs in common with students in these groups, they should not be viewed through the same lens.

Even some of the practices recommended by some experts to reduce mobility—such as urging parents to avoid school changes—don't apply to military families. They don't have the option of refusing to relocate. And because a transfer is usually to another state or another country, the parents can't simply provide their own transportation to keep their child in the same school.

MAJOR CHALLENGES FOR MILITARY STUDENTS IN SCHOOL

Listed below are major areas in which complications can arise during a school move for a military child. Keep in mind, however, that the more resources your school or district provides to help military families and students with these matters, the less likely these issues will lead to problems in your classroom.

Inconsistent Academic Standards: When a military student arrives in your class, it's likely that he or she has not learned some of the material that

> ## Military "Layoffs"
>
> Another transition that some military students may encounter is becoming a nonmilitary child. Cuts to the Department of Defense's budget and the withdrawal from Iraq are leading to a reduction in troop levels, meaning that some servicemen and women who intended to stay in the military until retirement are instead looking for new careers. Educators should be aware that this could be another life-altering event for a family, and one that could result in another school transfer for a child.

you have already covered this year. But it's also just as likely that the student has already mastered a skill or topic that your class has not learned yet.

This is because there is wide variation across states in what students are expected to know and when they are expected to know it. This mismatch between schools becomes even more critical as children enter high school and begin accumulating credits toward graduation. If courses or exams taken in one state are not accepted in another, students may not meet the requirements for graduation—even though they were on track to graduate in their previous school.

Extracurricular Activities: Students who participate in sports or other extracurricular activities, such as drama or chorus, often lose out on these activities when they relocate because they have missed try-outs or auditions, or because they do not meet eligibility criteria in their new school—even though these teams or activities are powerful vehicles for them to feel involved and make friendships in their new schools.

Special Education: Relocation can create a variety of challenges for a student with special needs. A student who had an individualized education program (IEP) or a 504 plan in his or her previous school may not automatically receive the same services in the new school. On the other hand, it's also possible that a child was labeled as a special education student in the last school because of problems related to having a parent in the military, and is considered a special education student in the new school for no good reason. Military family members with special needs are enrolled in the Exceptional Family Member Program, which is intended to make sure the individual's medical, emotional, or behavioral needs are met when a military member on active duty is transferred. Special education services vary, however, across civilian school districts. See our expanded section on Special Education in Chapter 3.

Parental Involvement: Just because parents are in the military does not mean they can't be involved in their child's education. In fact, surveys show that military parents are often very involved in school activities and support their children's education at home. You may need to recognize, however, that during times of deployment, the parent remaining at home may not be able to be as involved, or may need some flexibility regarding parent-teacher conferences, school events, and even homework.

Social Adjustment: A child who moves frequently may feel that he or she doesn't want to go to the trouble of making new friends again. Military students report that wondering where they will fit in and who they will eat lunch with can create tremendous stress.

CLASSROOM STRATEGIES

Here are suggestions on how you can make your classroom more responsive to the needs of military students. Many of these strategies are useful for any child who has frequently changed schools or who enters your class during the school year. But they are even more important for military students. Many of these suggestions don't require extra funding or staff, but they may be adjustments to how you organize your classroom. The extent to which you might need to use these strategies, however, depends on the answers to a few questions:

- Is your school located near a military base?
- How many students in your school or classroom are from military families?
- Are they significantly behind in meeting academic standards?

In addition, some of these responsibilities can be taken on by parent volunteers or high school and college students needing credit for service-learning projects.

We organize these strategies into three categories: When Military Students Arrive, While They Are in Your Class, and When They Leave. But some ideas will easily overlap into all three phases.

When Military Students Arrive

Quick Assessment: When new students arrive, have a quick diagnostic assessment prepared on your grade level or subject matter to determine how this child's skills and knowledge compare to the standards you are currently teaching in your class. Conduct the assessment in a comfortable, nonintimidating way within the child's first 2 days in the classroom to lessen the guesswork over the child's strengths and weaknesses. It's possible that your school already has a procedure in place for an initial screening assessment.

Language Assessments: If the child is an English learner, have a plan in place for quickly assessing the child's English language skills.

Student Records: A student's official records don't always transfer in a timely way. If you don't have time yourself to call the sending school to expedite the process, find out who in your school can follow through with this. These records can give you a baseline for how the child has performed academically, and might indicate whether performance dropped after another previous move. Past standardized test scores can provide a snapshot of how he or she is doing in core subject areas. Also pay close attention to any documents on health history and cognitive assessments, past Special Education eligibility or IEPs to see how this child has progressed over time.

Viewing Their Work: If a new student brings along past work or a portfolio from a previous school, take a look at it. You might get some good ideas. Asking him or her about a favorite assignment or project could also help you form a connection with the student.

Meeting the Parents: Don't wait until scheduled parent-teacher conference time to meet the child's parents or give them a phone call. Even a quick, 10-minute phone conversation can shed light on the child's learning style, interests, or any other information that may help make the child's first few days or weeks in your class a little more comfortable. Chances are the parents are eager for you to know something about their child.

Having a Welcoming Classroom: Establish an expectation in your classroom that new students will be included in activities in both the classroom and at recess or lunch breaks. Pinpoint the students in your class that are the most likely to be friendly to a new student during the first few days, and ask them to assist the new student in finding classroom materials, learning the routines, and meeting other students. It might be especially helpful if this child is one who has changed schools because of a family move in the past, or is a military-connected child. This practice can be in addition to any "buddy" programs that the school may already have in place.

Classroom Rules: Establish high expectations for behavior in your classroom, but make sure your rules, and any consequences that come with breaking the rules, are clearly communicated to the new student. Be cognizant that what was permitted in the child's previous school might not be allowed in your classroom, so be understanding during the first few weeks.

Clearly Communicating Attendance Policies: Adjusting to a new school—once again—can take an emotional toll on military students. Watch for repeated absences and tardiness during those initial weeks after the student's arrival. Missing days of school can make gaps in learning even worse. Make sure the student and parents are quickly made aware of your policies regarding homework and missed class work. But also have procedures in place for allowing students to make up work if they miss school. The chances are good that some of the rules in place at the child's previous school are different than yours. (Also see Block Leave in Chapter 4.)

Contacting the Previous School: If the child's records don't provide sufficient details on his or her school performance, make a phone call or send an e-mail to the child's previous teacher or counselor to see if you can gather some additional background information.

Keeping Extra Supplies: Parents may not have time to purchase school supplies in the midst of a move, and your class or school probably requires different materials and supplies than the student's last school. Even if they brought their old supplies, they might still be packed up in a box. Have a starter kit with paper, pens and pencils, erasers, folders, notebooks—even a backpack—so there are no delays for students in doing their assignments. If possible, have extra copies of workbooks or textbooks so the student won't have to share with someone.

In the News

The *Fort Hood Sentinel* featured a unique project in which 200 students living on base experienced their own mock deployment to better understand what their parents go through when they are sent on a military mission.

The children, ages 3 to 18, learned about Iraq and Afghanistan, and went through a mock "readiness processing" where they received eye examinations, tried on tactical gear, and practiced marching. They also received "dog tags," field journals, canteens, compasses, and badges with their name, rank, and platoon assignment.

According to the paper, the exercise was intended to help "demystify" the deployment process and alleviate the fears some children have when their military parent is deployed.

The day ended with a "reintegration," in which parents and siblings welcomed home their "deployed" family members with signs, hugs, and lots of picture-taking.

Even though this event was held on a base, something similar could be done with a classroom at a school where military parents are frequently deployed.

While They Are in Your Class

The Need for Tutoring: If learning gaps do exist, if the child is performing below grade level, or if the child's grades seem to be dropping from his or her previous school, be aware of all opportunities that your school or district provides to help students catch up—both during the school day and in before- or after-school programs. If your school is a Title I school, the student may also qualify for free private tutoring through the Supplemental Educational Services provision of No Child Left Behind (NCLB). As you will see in sections below, there are additional resources designed to help military students. Military bases, school liaison officers, and many other organizations provide information, tutoring, and other support to military students who need help to maximize their academic potential.

Choice of Materials: Find ways to integrate military history, literature written by a military family member, websites, or other material with a military family's perspective into your teaching. However, be careful not to single a military child out when this content is being discussed in class. A military child may feel uncomfortable being singled out or expected to be a cultural ambassador.

Curriculum Materials

The following are examples of publications that could be used to integrate the experiences of military students into language arts assignments or other content areas.

- *My Story: Blogs by Four Military Teens,* by Michelle D. Sherman and DeAnne M. Sherman. The booklet presents the blog entries of four fictional teenagers as they write about their relationships with their military parents.
- *Finding My Way: A Teen's Guide to Living with a Parent Who Has Experienced Trauma,* by Michelle D. Sherman and DeAnne M. Sherman. The book includes lessons, activities and resources aimed at teens.
- *While You Are Away,* by Eileen Spinelli. This picture book is appropriate for younger children. Three children, speaking in the first person, anticipate the returns of their parents, who are away on active military duty.
- *A Boy at War,* by Harry Mazer. This novel is appropriate for students in grades 5–9. It tells the story of a 14-year-old boy whose father is an officer assigned to the USS Arizona when the attack on Pearl Harbor takes place in 1941.

Having Frequent Contact with the Parents: If the child will be missing school due to a military parent's scheduled leave—also known as block leave—it's wise to meet or talk with the parent before that period to make schoolwork expectations clear. When conferences are scheduled, or when additional conversations with parents are necessary, learn how to use Skype or other video conferencing tools in order to connect with deployed parents. When class plays, performances, or a student's special presentation occurs, see if the child wants you to record video of it for the parent who is away.

Enrichment: If a student has demonstrated that he or she has already mastered the material you are teaching, have a plan for allowing them to move to the next level or to do more in-depth work on the topic, such as an independent project or research. They can even share what they learn with the class.

Facebook: Some teachers may still have mixed feelings about students using social networking sites, but teens are now far more likely to use them than e-mail. Safeguards are in place and Facebook can allow students to stay in touch with friends they have left behind or who have left them. Teachers can also create their own pages as a way to connect with and support students who move on, as long as they are in compliance with district or school policies.

Creating Bulletin Boards: Teachers with military students in their classes—or any students that have come from other parts of the United States or the world—can prepare bulletin boards with maps to show where students have lived. Teachers with interactive whiteboards in their classrooms can use Google Earth or other online tools to present the same information. In schools with a large military representation, teachers have sometimes created "hero walls" to allow students to honor their family members serving in the military.

Having Classroom Helpers: If your students have certain jobs or responsibilities in the class, don't hesitate to give the new student an assignment, whether it's walking with a classmate to deliver something to the office, or helping to push in the chairs at the end of the day. This can make the child feel involved.

Holding Morning Meetings: More common in elementary grades than at the middle and high school level, morning meetings can set the tone for the day, allow students to share news or comments with their peers, and prepare the class for the academic work of the day ahead. Such meetings may be especially helpful when you know that military students in your class are facing an event such as large deployment or if a military-related tragedy has occurred. More information on organizing and using morning meetings is available from http://responsiveclassroom.org/.

A Hero Wall at Santa Margarita Elementary in Oceanside, California

Photo by Rashell Parkhurst

Providing Instruction in a Variety of Ways: You may not know the method of instruction that is most helpful for new students in your class, so use a variety of formats, including small, cooperative groups with assigned roles and responsibilities, individual work, peer learning, and whole-group discussions or lectures. Allowing students to work in small groups may also create more opportunities for the new student to get to know classmates and feel comfortable asking questions.

Fostering Friendships: Friendships can't be forced, but observe whether the child is beginning to make some connections with students in the school. Also, check to see with whom they are associating—students who are

---

In the News

The *Topeka Capital-Journal* featured a project at Shawnee Heights Middle School in which students interviewed military veterans at a senior living facility to hear first-hand reports of what it was like to serve during a war. The students' interviews were part of a performance-based learning project called "Unsung Military Heroes."

According to the article, Donna Sanders, the school's enrichment coordinator, said the project was a great opportunity for students to hear stories from World War II.

"These veterans are a great resource, and these stories won't be told forever," Sanders said.

positive role models or those that might encourage risky behavior. If is the latter, further intervention may be needed.

Political Statements: Regardless of whether or not you agree with a particular mission that the military is sent on by our government leaders, refrain from commenting about whether missions are justified or unjustified. Your mission is to make sure the child progresses and feels supported while he or she is in your class.

Learning from the Child: A military child has probably lived some-where else that you and your other students have not–possibly even overseas. During classroom discussions or morning meetings, incorporate the child's experiences and knowledge into the conversation. Be aware that some students, for a variety of reasons, may not want to talk about past experiences, or would prefer to share in a small group or in a one-on-one situation.

Extracurricular Activities: Find out whether the child was involved in any extracurricular activities in their previous community, and make sure

---

Pen Pals

When the father of one of Dale Borgeson's 3rd grade students at Vintage Hills Elementary was deployed at sea for most of the school year, the teacher thought of a way to keep not only the sailor's daughter—but also the other students in the class—in touch with the members of the military. The students in his class at the Temecula, California school became pen pals with crewmembers on the USS Rentz.

"The crewmen did a great job of writing to the class on a regular basis," Borgeson says.

When the ship returned, the girl's father and two other crewmembers visited the class. They also donated a plaque and a flag that is still in the school office.

"This experience helped me become much more aware of the needs of our military families," Borgeson says. "I was happy to have had a way to contribute, in a small way, to our military mission."

the parents and the child have information on how to sign up for programs. Classes, sports, or other activities can assist the student in developing friendships and can help to ease the stress related to relocating or a parent's deployment. A coach or an instructor can also play the important role of giving a military child another adult to talk to and monitor how the child is adjusting.

Utilizing School Support Teams: If you find a military child is struggling academically, socially, or emotionally, use existing school support structures, like a Student Success Team. These are ways for teachers, the principal, the parent, and other school staff to sit together to address individual student needs, challenges, and strengths with the ultimate goal of creating an action plan. Or, if you have common planning time with other grade-level or content-area teachers, share your concerns and ask for feedback.

When They Leave

Preparing for the Next Move: Sometimes transfers happen unexpectedly, and there is little time to prepare. Help the child maintain a portfolio of their best work—such as essays, tests, artwork, photos of projects, or videos of presentations to the class—so they have something they can show to their next teacher. It might not be part of the child's official academic record, but it can help them communicate what they have been working on and demonstrate their abilities.

Adding a Letter to the Child's File: Official report cards can't tell the next school everything about a student. You might want to write a letter to the new school describing the student, especially if there are any particular strategies that you found successful or lessons that the child found especially engaging. This information could help the new teacher form a connection with the student.

Talking with the Parents: Give the parents a sense of where their child stands academically before they depart for a new school. Offer suggestions for what the student should be working on if they are going to be out of school temporarily during the transition, or point them to websites that could provide extra practice for their grade level.

RESEARCH HIGHLIGHTS ON STUDENT MOBILITY

Below are some key findings on student mobility in general and on military students.

The SETS Project

The Secondary Education Transition Study—a joint project between the Army and the Military Child Education Coalition (MCEC)—documented the effects of school transition specifically for high school students. Released in 2001, the study showed wide variation in how schools handle the transfer and interpretation of student records. Inconsistencies in school schedules and calendars increased the chances of problematic transitions.

Solutions recommended included allowing parents to hand carry student records to make sure they arrive with the student, having virtual tours of schools or new student orientations online, and providing options for enhanced or alternate diplomas and earning graduation credit.

MCEC is currently updating the study with new research.

- In a 2008 study, Diana H. Gruman from Western Washington University found that the most important factor in a new student's adjustment to school is the teacher(s). Those who were supportive of highly mobile students had a strong influence on their attitudes toward school and on their behavior in the classroom. The researchers recommended intensive tutoring for new students struggling to overcome academic challenges and professional development for teachers so they can better understand the unique circumstances faced by mobile students.
- A 1993 study by Dr. David Wood, at the time a professor of pediatrics at Cedars-Sinai Medical Center in Los Angeles, showed that children who changed schools at least six times between 1st and 12th grade were 35% more likely to fail a grade than children who didn't change schools or those who had only moved a couple of times during that period.
- The University of Chicago's David Kerbow wrote in 2003 that highly mobile students were an average of 4 months behind their less transient classmates on standardized tests by 4th grade. By the 6th grade, students who were highly mobile during elementary school lagged behind their classmates by as much as a full year.
- More recently, a study from researchers at the University of Michigan (Burkam, Lee, & Dwyer, 2009) used data from the Early Childhood Longitudinal Study–Kindergarten Cohort, a large sample of over 30,000 children, to examine the impact of mobility on children in the early grades. In the full sample, changing schools does

not appear to have serious detrimental effects on children's learning. However, examining effects by certain groups showed that children of lower socioeconomic status face greater academic setbacks when they change schools during kindergarten, but those who repeat kindergarten may show learning gains when they change schools. Children who are receiving special education services typically do worse after they change schools.

- In 2010, Catherine P. Bradshaw and colleagues from Johns Hopkins University found that adolescents from military families experience significant stress related to making school transitions, from worrying about maintaining past friendships and forming new ones, to feeling lost in class because they haven't covered certain material. In focus groups, students talked about learning how to "blend in" to new social situations and seeking out other military students. School staff members interviewed commented that military students in high school appear more mature than other students their age.

- Allan M. O'Brien (2007) from the Peabody College for Teachers at Vanderbilt University examined the relationship between mobility and achievement in a New York school district adjacent to the Fort Drum Army base. About half of the district's 4,000 students are military children. The study showed that while mobility can have negative effects on military children's performance, outcomes significantly improve when children have "rich social support networks." This can include the attitudes of parents—especially mothers—regarding the move and whether information is available about the school and community where the child is going.

RESOURCES FOCUSING ON MILITARY CHILDREN

Listed below are organizations, programs and publications that can provide greater insight into many of the issues that students from military families face.

Military Child Education Coalition (MCEC): This is a worldwide organization focused on ensuring quality educational opportunities for all military-connected children affected by mobility, family separation, and transition. The MCEC performs research, develops resources, conducts professional institutes and conferences, and publishes resources for all constituencies. http://www.militarychild.org/

Department of Defense Education Activity: A field activity of the Office of the Secretary of Defense, DoDEA operates schools for the children of military members stationed at bases in both the United States and overseas. This website provides information on current initiatives within the schools, an overview of curriculum, a data center, and links to all 194 schools. http://www.dodea.edu/home/about.cfm

Building Resilient Kids: This online Internet course from Johns Hopkins University is designed to help school administrators, teachers, and faculty to be more aware of the special needs of children who come from military families. http://www.jhsph.edu/mci/training_course/

School Connectedness: Improving Students' Lives: As part of the Military Child Initiative at the Johns Hopkins University Bloomberg School of Public Health, three publications discuss practices that can help students feel more connected to their schools. There is a monograph, an executive summary, and a tip sheet for teachers. http://www.jhsph.edu/mci/resources/School_Connectedness

Tackling Tough Topics: An Educator's Guide to Working with Military Kids: This booklet was developed by the Washington State Office of the Superintendent of Public Instruction. https://www.operationmilitarykids.org/resources/ToughTopics%20BookletFINAL.pdf

Military Family Research Institute: Located at Purdue University, the MFRI is a research and outreach organization focusing on quality of life issues for military families. http://www.cfs.purdue.edu/mfri/public/default.aspx

Military Students on the Move: A Toolkit for School Leaders: This manual is written for school leaders, but also provides valuable information for teachers on how to help their military-impacted students cope with relocation and make the transition process easier for students and their families. http://hanscomservices.com/graphics/School%20Liaison/PDFs/A-Toolkit-for-School-Leaders_2012.pdf

Leveling the Playing Field for Military Connected Students: This PowerPoint presentation provides a brief overview of the issues military children face and ways schools can respond. http://www.militaryk12partners.dodea.edu/docs/reference_leveling.pdf

Operation Military Kids: This handout, focusing on students whose parents are in the National Guard and Reserves, provides a quick overview to help educators become sensitive to the unique culture of military children and their families. http://www.extension.umn.edu/FamilyRelations/components/OMK_LC_handout.pdf

Handbook for Garrison Commanders and Reference for School Superintendents: An MCEC publication, this handbook focuses specifically on the Army and is a useful primer for school leaders needing to understand more about how the military functions and about why a "disconnect" between civilian schools and military families exists. Search for it in MCEC's online Library at http://www.militarychild.org/library

Special Education Professional Development: As part of its Partnership Program, DoDEA has created training modules for educators in civilian schools focusing on issues such as autism, conducting special education assessments, and Response to Intervention. http://www.militaryk12partners.dodea.edu/resources.cfm?colId=sped

Student Mobility: This is a thoughtful collection of research highlights and suggested recommendations from the Leon County Schools in Florida. http://www.tandl.leon.k12.fl.us/programme/mobility.html

Students at the Center: This guide from DoDEA's Military K–12 Partners website speaks to the various groups involved in helping military students be successful: parents, civilian school officials, and military leaders. The section for educators includes information on the military branches, the Impact Aid program, and basic military terms. http://www.militaryk12partners.dodea.edu/studentsAtTheCenter/index.html

BRATS: Our Journey Home: This documentary, featuring Kris Kristofferson and Norman Schwarzkopf, provides a glimpse into the experiences of children who have grown up in military households. Brats Without Borders, the nonprofit organization that produced the film, has an outreach effort, Operation Military Brat, which offers workshops to educators and other groups to raise awareness about what it's like to grow up as a military child. http://www.bratsourjourneyhome.com/index.htm

Building Capacity in Military-Connected Schools: A part of the DoDEA project at USC that led to the creation of this guidebook, this website provides information on programs for military students, ongoing research, videos, and newsletters featuring practices that public schools can implement to help military children and families feel more welcome and supported. http://buildingcapacity.usc.edu/

CHAPTER 3

Policy Issues

This chapter focuses on the role of policy in supporting the education of military students. As a teacher, you may not spend a lot of time thinking about federal or state legislation. But it can be useful to know where your state and district stands on adopting or implementing some of these policies, and how they can address the needs of military students in your classroom.

Topics covered in this chapter are:

- Lessons from Federal Programs for Highly Mobile Students
- Common Core State Standards
- Common Education Data Standards
- Supporting Military Students with Special Needs
- The Interstate Compact on Educational Opportunity for Military Children
- Lessons from DoDEA Schools

LESSONS FROM FEDERAL PROGRAMS FOR HIGHLY MOBILE STUDENTS

The education community can learn from practices and policies designed to meet the needs of other students facing frequent transitions. For example, the McKinney-Vento Homeless Education Assistance Act requires schools to have a liaison to ensure that homeless students are enrolled in school–even if all required documents are not available–and that homeless students and their families receive appropriate services. Similarly, schools with large proportions of military children can designate a staff member or volunteer as a liaison–someone who becomes familiar with common pressing issues and has the knowledge or the connections with other agencies to resolve problems. This person can be the primary contact for the School Liaison Officers who work for the branches of the military.

Randy Garcia, the director of pupil services for the Escondido Union School District, looks to McKinney-Vento as a model for serving military families by:

- providing a liaison to better connect them with the school and help them receive tutoring, counseling, medical care, housing, and other resources
- allowing students to remain in their school even if their parent moves or is deployed to ensure a consistent and stable learning environment
- allowing families to choose their preferred school through a School of Choice process
- adopting a school board policy and administrative regulation explaining how military students will be served and supported throughout the district

As another example, the Migrant Student Records Exchange Initiative–part of the No Child Left Behind Act–created a system in which states can share educational and health information on migrant children who move between states and, as a result, have official records in more than one state. The technology facilitates school enrollment and grade placement, and makes sure students receive credit for courses taken–all of which are issues that military children also encounter. The purpose of the program is to "ensure greater continuity of educational services for migrant children by providing a mechanism for all states to exchange education-related information on migrant children who move from state to state due to their migratory lifestyle," according to the Department of Education. The system also allows states to notify each other when a migrant student is moving to a different state. Such a system would also be valuable for schools receiving large numbers of military students. An effort to create Common Education Data Standards, launched by a consortium of organizations including the Council of Chief State School Officers and the Data Quality Campaign, has similar goals–allowing educators to quickly understand a student's academic performance in order to keep the student moving forward. (See section on Common Education Data Standards later in this chapter.)

COMMON CORE STATE STANDARDS

When military children attend one of the 194 DoDEA schools around the world–whether it's McBride Elementary on Ft. Benning in Georgia or Boeblingen Elementary in Heidelberg, Germany–they are taught the same curriculum, and are assessed using the same tests, which allows for comparisons among students.

This uniformity is in place so that military children, who often must pick up and change schools with little advance preparation, won't fall behind in school, or conversely have to repeat material that they've already mastered.

This creates a predictable situation for families who tend to have unpredictable lives.

Currently in the United States, each state sets its own standards for what students are expected to learn as they progress through school. But this system has led to wide variation across the country, and students—not just those in the military, but anyone who moves from state to state—sometimes experience redundancy in lessons or far worse, miss out on entire subjects.

The Common Core State Standards is an effort led by two national organizations—the Council of Chief State School Officers and the National Governors Association—to develop clear and consistent guidelines for what students are expected to learn and to prepare them for college and careers.

The Common Core, in effect, mirrors the approach already used by the DoDEA schools. Supporters of the Common Core, which the Obama administration is urging states to adopt, say that in addition to allowing for comparison of student performance across the country, the Core also makes it easier for educators to share best practices about instruction.

Accommodating the needs of military students—and other highly mobile populations—was actually part of the rationale behind the development of the Common Core.

In a letter of endorsement, Mary M. Keller, the president and CEO of the Military Child Education Coalition, wrote about why the initiative makes sense for military students.

> As military assignments or family circumstances resulting from a parent's deployment lead to school moves, parents and students need to be confident that these transitions will not increase turbulence in students' lives or endanger their opportunity to achieve. They also need to know that no matter where they attend school, they will have the chance to master those concepts and skills that ensure successful study at the post-secondary level and prepare them to enter the world of work.

Obviously, if all U.S. states adopt the Common Core standards, this would address many of the obstacles that military children moving between installations in the United States currently face, such as repeating or missing academic material and transferring credit for courses taken.

But that may or may not happen. At the time of publication,45 states had adopted the Common Core.

And even if they did, the Common Core at this point only includes standards in math and English/language arts and doesn't address social studies, science, or other subjects.

Nevertheless, the Common Core standards provide some solutions for military students—and others who relocate often—that can minimize the disruption in their educational progress.

COMMON EDUCATION DATA STANDARDS

Military families are keenly aware that states and even local school districts vary tremendously on the information they require when a new student enrolls in school. But clearly military families are not the only ones who move from state to state and have to cope with record-keeping procedures that were different in their previous school.

That's why the Common Education Data Standards (CEDS) initiative was launched—to create a core set of preschool, K–12 and K–12 to postsecondary variables that could be easily compared and understood from state to state. One presentation by the initiative describes it as creating "an integrated profile of each learner that can be passed seamlessly" among institutions and between states.

Partners in the effort include the National Center for Education Statistics, several state and local education agencies, the Council of Chief State School Officers, State Higher Education Executive Officers, and other organizations that focus on education data.

One example given to emphasize the need for common data standards is Hurricane Katrina, after which thousands of students dispersed to other states and districts across the South, creating a pressing need for administrators and teachers in their new schools to quickly and accurately obtain their records and place them in classes appropriately. This scenario is nothing new for military parents and students.

The CEDS effort is voluntary and is still a work in progress. While it wasn't designed solely with military families in mind, it is a response to many of the complications they face when changing schools on short notice.

To learn more about the initiative and what you can do to move it forward, visit: http://commoneddatastandards.org/

SUPPORTING MILITARY STUDENTS
WITH SPECIAL NEEDS

Changing schools frequently is difficult for all military families. The experience can present even more challenges for students with special needs.

IDEA and the IEP

The Individuals with Disabilities Education Act (IDEA) mandates that students with disabilities who qualify for specialized services be provided with a free and appropriate education in the least restrictive environment. Under the IDEA, a parent along with a team of educators draft a student's individualized educational program (IEP). An IEP documents a student's disability eligibility status and school- and classroom-based supports, such as testing accommodations, annual academic goals, and other specialized services (e.g., for speech and language). The IDEA requires that an IEP team, which is composed of a parent, teachers, a school administrator, and other credentialed or designated instructional services staff, such as an occupational therapist, draft a new IEP at least annually and make a comprehensive evaluation every 3 years.

In addition, parents have the right to call for changes to an existing IEP or to call a meeting to discuss drafting a new plan if they feel the services their child is receiving need to change.

For military families, this entire process is repeated multiple times and educators in one district may not always see the situation the same way as those in the child's previous school. Realize as well that military children often face increased stress and trauma that may result in poor learning and behavior outcomes. Educators and other professionals should consider these factors when determining whether a child requires special services.

Timely and Accurate Information

Making sure schools receive as much information as possible in a timely manner is a key to ensuring that military students are served appropriately. Some school districts such as the Los Angeles Unified School District utilize a secured online system to track current and past IEPs. These tracking systems assist schools in identifying incoming students with IEPs and monitoring the progress of current students with IEPs. However, not all school districts have an online tracking system, and often, incoming students with IEPs are not identified. More school districts—especially those serving highly mobile students—should implement such a model. In addition, numerous steps can be taken to make sure there is a smooth transition between schools. When enrolling a new student, school officials should routinely ask whether the student has any special needs or had an IEP in their previous school. Under the IDEA policy, parents can call an IEP meeting during the first 30 days of the student's attendance at the new school, but with so many issues to take care of during a move—especially if one parent is deployed—the family may not get to this important task.

When the meeting is held, a new IEP can be drafted to fit the student's needs within the school's existing programs. In addition, when families are leaving your district, you can assist them in the process by contacting the new school with information about the child's needs.

The Exceptional Family Member Program

School officials should also become familiar with the military's Exceptional Family Member Program (EFMP), in which the needs of military family members requiring special medical, developmental, emotional, or other services are considered when a serviceman or woman is transferred. Military members on active duty are required to enroll in this program, but it is independent from school special education programs and there may be limited communication between the two—especially in communities not located near a military installation.

Some installations have an EFMP liaison that assists families with enrolling in the program and making sure their family member receives the services they need. This person can work in tandem with a school district's special education director on behalf of students with special needs. As a teacher you may want to ask whether such a liaison is available to your school, so that you can work together to help students in your class who have special needs.

In addition, there are a variety of resources available to inform both educators and parents about making sure military-connected students with special needs receive the best care and education possible.

- **STOMP**, which stands for Specialized Training of Military Parents, is a nationwide parent training and information center for military families. The project aims to "empower military parents, individuals with disabilities, and service providers with knowledge, skills, and resources so that they might access services to create a collaborative environment for family and professional partnerships without regard to geographic location." One component of President Obama's "Strengthening Our Military Families" directive is to continue the implementation of the STOMP initiative: http://www.stompproject.org/
- **The MilitaryHOMEFRONT** website provides a listing of EFMP/special needs contacts for all military installations both in the United States and overseas: http://www.militaryhomefront.dod.mil/portal/page/mhf/MHF/MHF_DETAIL_1?section_id=20.40.500.570.0.0.0.0.0&content_id=180334
- **"Understanding the Special Education Process as a Military Parent"** is a four-part guide available on the MilitaryOneSource.mil website. Click on Career & Education, Special Needs in Education and Advocating in the Schools. http://www.militaryonesource.mil

THE INTERSTATE COMPACT ON EDUCATIONAL OPPORTUNITY FOR MILITARY CHILDREN

Unlike their civilian peers, children from military families change schools almost every 3 years, the consequences of which vary depending on the age and level of the child. For example, at the kindergarten level, military

The Interstate Compact on Educational Opportunity for Military Children is designed to facilitate or provide for:

- the timely enrollment of children [from] military families and [ensure] that they are not placed at a disadvantage due to difficulty in the transfer of education records between schools or variations in entrance/age requirements
- the student placement process through which children of military families are not disadvantaged by variations in attendance requirements, scheduling, sequencing, grading, course content, or assessment
- the qualification and eligibility for enrollment, educational programs, and participation in extracurricular academic, athletic, and social activities
- the on-time graduation of children of military families
- promulgation and enforcement of administrative rules implementing the provisions of [the] compact
- for the uniform collection and sharing of information between and among member states, schools and military families under [the] compact
- coordination between this compact and other compacts affecting military children
- flexibility and coordination between the educational system, parents and the student in order to achieve educational success for the student

Source: Council of State Governments, 2008

children may begin the school year in one state, where the enrollment guidelines allow a student to enter kindergarten just after turning 5. But then they might transfer mid-year to a school in a state with a much earlier cut-off date for turning 5—suddenly making the child too young for kindergarten.

In the early grades, differences in state policy, while problematic, are to a degree benign. As military children progress in school, however, the stakes associated with ill-aligned policies become higher and produce dire consequences for children from military families. For example, to earn a high school diploma, many states require that graduating seniors complete a course in state history (e.g., California state history in California). Military children who begin their senior year in one state and transfer to a high school in a different state may not fulfill that requirement in time to earn their high school diploma—a reality that may limit their postsecondary opportunities.

Prior to April 2008, states lacked a uniform policy to address the needs of military children in transition. Issues related to enrollment, course/program placement, eligibility, and graduations were generally addressed on a case-by-case basis. While the Department of Defense had long worked with individual school districts, primarily those with high military enrollments, to reduce the difficulties associated with student transition, stakeholders and policymakers agreed that much more could and needed to be done at both the state and local level. They hoped that once enacted, an interstate compact—a contractual agreement entered into by two or more states in areas that are traditionally protected by state sovereignty (e.g., on education policy)—would supersede conflicting state laws related to the transition of military children from school to school and across state lines.

The purpose of the Interstate Compact on Educational Opportunity for Military Children is to reduce and/or eliminate "barriers to educational success" for children from military families as they transition between schools and across state lines.

The compact also provides for the creation of individual state councils and an interstate commission. According to the Council of State Governments (2008), unless otherwise specified, the Interstate Compact applies to the children of:

- active duty military personnel
- members of the uniformed services, including the four main branches as well as the Commissioned Corps of the National Oceanic and Atmospheric Administration, and Public Health Services
- veterans of the uniformed services who are "medically discharged or retired" up to "one year after medical discharge or retirement"
- "members of the uniformed services who" are deceased as a result of their service within the past year.

As of this writing, 39 states have endorsed the Interstate Compact. While the responsiveness of states to the compact is a positive development, implementing it at the local level has been challenging. An organizational structure, however, is emerging and continues to evolve. Despite having endorsed this legislation, some states have done so only symbolically and have not informed district superintendents and/or school personnel of the compact's policy implications. In the absence of state action, however, some districts have begun to implement their own policies to ease the transition of military children.

As a teacher to military children, you may want to inquire whether your state has endorsed the Interstate Compact. It's also important to find out whether your district or school has developed any policies, practices, and resources designed to ease academic transitions of military children.

Broadly conceived, the goal of the Interstate Compact is to provide systemic support to military children in the areas that have historically been problematic for these families—enrollment, placement, eligibility, and gradu-ation. Gaps in the dissemination of information and implementation, howev-er, hinder the ability of civilian public schools to provide consistent support to military children. Moving forward, greater awareness and understanding of the compact is needed. School officials can support this process by learn-ing more about the compact, its policy implications, and the resources that are available. For more information on the Interstate Compact, visit www.mic3.net.

[The above material is an excerpt from M. C. Esqueda, R. A. Astor, & K. De Pedro (2012). A call to duty: Educational policy and school reform ad-dressing the needs of children from military families. *Educational Researcher, 41*(2), 65–70.]

LESSONS FROM DoDEA SCHOOLS

With 194 schools in 14 countries, Department of Defense Education Activ-ity schools were created to respond to the specific needs of highly mobile military children. But that doesn't mean civilian school districts with military students can't learn from some of their practices.

DoDEA schools have been recognized for having high overall achieve-ment, regularly scoring above the national average on the National Assess-ment of Educational Progress. While gaps do exist in performance between Black and White students and Hispanic and White students, the gaps are smaller than in regular public schools.

But this system—roughly the size of a large urban school district—achieves these results in spite of experiencing high student turnover, an average of about 37% a year. There are also other statistics to consider:

- While the educational levels of enlisted personnel have been increasing, parents of DoDEA students are generally not highly educated or highly paid. The majority of DoDEA students have a parent who is an enlisted member of the military, not an officer.
- DoD Domestic Dependent Elementary and Secondary Schools, the domestic system, has a larger percentage of minority students than their public school counterparts. But their students still score above the national average in reading and writing.

The question for teachers: How do DoDEA schools help military students to be successful in spite of the complicated lives that many of them lead?

In their 2003 study, "It's a Way of Life for Us: High Mobility and High Achievement in Department of Defense Schools," Vanderbilt University re-searchers Claire E. Smrekar and Debra E. Owens suggest that DoDEA has created a culture of high expectations for students that is complemented by treating high mobility as "'a way of life' rather than an intractable problem."

"The foundation of institutional and community stability in the DoDEA system includes several structural supports—some that represent effective levers for educational policymakers and others that signal unique features of the military community," they write.

Accessible Student Records

For schools with high student turnover, the timely transfer of student records poses one of the greatest challenges to making sure students have a smooth transition into a new school. DoDEA schools have created a standardized process to ensure that there is as little delay as possible in students' learning.

"We put a lot of focus on trying to get a lot of information to the next school before the student arrives," says Mike Lynch, the chief of policy and legislation at DoDEA.

At the elementary level, parents carry their child's official records by hand to the next school, while the sending school keeps a copy.

At the middle and high school level, a student's transcript is electronically transferred to the receiving school—allowing for no interruption in educational services.

DoDEA schools have also worked to eliminate what Lynch calls "homegrown" forms—those locally created documents or permission slips that schools often require in order for students to be enrolled.

Lynch adds that when a student is transferring to another DoDEA school, teachers or school administrators often communicate with the receiving school if they think there is a particular educational or adjustment issue that could create problems for the child at the new school.

Communication between DoDEA and civilian schools when a child is transferring from one to the other is not that common, however. He described this communication as "episodic, random, and rare."

Finally, the fact that all DoDEA schools use the same curriculum helps to ensure that students won't fall behind during a move—even if they are in one DoDEA school in Germany on a Friday and enter another one in North Carolina the following Monday.

Supportive School Climates

DoDEA schools also build their school climate around the fact that students—and parents—are always on the move.

When a student comes in to a DoDEA school to register, the schools actually prefer that the student wait a day or two to come to school, explains

Patricia A. Cassiday, the former coordinator for counseling and psychological services for DoDEA.

That gives the teacher time to get a desk, books, and other materials ready for the student. It also gives the class a chance to prepare to welcome the new student. The scene is more of a "celebration instead of 'oh no, another student,'" Cassiday says.

An appointment with the school counselor is usually scheduled as soon as the student is enrolled.

In the classroom, teachers are trained to differentiate instruction to meet students' individual learning needs. Even though all DoDEA schools use the same curriculum, many students have still been in a variety of classrooms and through different experiences that could affect whether they are meeting the standards for their grade.

If a large deployment takes place, the school community will often hold a barbecue or some other event for the families. This is not only a way to recognize the servicemen and women, but also allows the schools to see how the spouses remaining behind are handling the transition. They might say they don't need support, Cassiday says, but they will attend something that is organized for their children.

Then, when a child is preparing to move on, the class or school offers some gesture to make the student feel as if they were appreciated. It can be as simple as a certificate, a T-shirt, or a pillowcase signed by all of student's classmates. It's a way to say, "thank you for being part of our school community," Cassiday says.

CHAPTER 4

Deployment

Deployment refers to the assignment of an individual or a military unit to a location away from the home base for a task or a mission. A military service member can be deployed for a training exercise, peacekeeping mission, or to the middle of a war zone, so each deployment carries a unique set of circumstances that can affect the military member's children in different ways.

At a minimum, children experience a range of emotions and behaviors related to being separated from a parent for an extended period of time. That separation is compounded, however, by the fear that their parent could be in danger, could return with an injury, or might not return at all.

Some experts have observed that there are several emotional phases that families might also experience in relationship to the deployment cycle (Amen, Jellen, Merves, & Lee, 1988). For example, the pre-deployment phase can create tremendous anger and anxiety for children as they count down the days until their parent will be leaving. Alternately, some children might begin to withdraw from their deploying parent as they try to brace themselves for daily life without him or her. Deployment can leave a child feeling disorganized. The "reintegration" or reunion phase can be joyful, but also confusing—especially during a time of war—when a child realizes that his or her parent is somehow different than before the deployment.

Be aware of the various—and sometimes unpredictable—ways that the deployment experience can affect military students' behavior in school and the attention they give to their academic work. You can create a warm and caring school climate that helps students through such difficult periods in their lives.

The Deployment Cycle

The cycle of deployment for a member of the military is described as having three main phases, each of which affect children in different ways:

- *Pre-deployment*—the notification that the military parent will be deployed
- *Deployment*—the period of time that the military parent is away
- *Post-deployment*—the return of the military parent, often also referred to as "reintegration"

THE WARS IN IRAQ AND AFGHANISTAN

The extended conflicts in Iraq and Afghanistan have presented opportunities for better understanding how children respond to the deployment of a parent. Since 2001, approximately two million military children have experienced a parent's deployment, according to DoDEA.

In addition, roughly 500,000 children—more than a third of all children with parents in the military—have been born into military families since the beginning of the war. For them, the potential that a parent will be deployed and put in harm's way has always been the norm. See the Research Highlights on Parental Deployment section later in this chapter.

MAJOR ISSUES RELATED TO DEPLOYMENT

The way a child responds to a parent's deployment can be unique to each child and the dynamics of his or her family. There are some overarching issues, however, that you should be aware of as you try to provide a stable classroom environment for children during an unstable period in their lives.

Changing Roles in the Family: Possibly the most disruptive aspect of a parent's deployment is that the family members remaining behind must take on responsibilities that the deployed parent handled while he or she was home. For children, who tend to rely on routines and structure, this can be especially upsetting. Additional household chores or responsibilities, such as taking care of younger siblings, can shift to older children and affect whether they are getting their schoolwork done or maintaining their involvement in extracurricular activities. When a single parent is deployed, the upheaval can be even greater. Children might have to move in with family friends or relatives.

Block Leave: This is a period of time in the midst of a deployment—generally about 2 weeks—that a member of the military is allowed to return home to spend time with family members. Military students in your class may wish to stay home so they can spend time with their parent on leave. School districts with a large number of military families may already have a written policy outlining how many excused absences during this leave are allowed and the options students have for completing schoolwork at home during that time or making up missed assignments. If not, prepare in advance for these periods. Block leave should be viewed as a valuable time for the child to reconnect with the parent. Consider, however, the individual student's performance. Is he or she caught up in class and generally responsible for turning in work completed at home? Or is he or she already behind and days out of school might make matters worse? In addition, parents may also expect that children should be excused from school on the day a parent leaves for a deployment or on the day the military parent's unit returns. These are other days to discuss in advance.

Financial Stress: If the parent being deployed is the one who paid all the bills, handled car maintenance, and managed other financial matters for the family, the parent left at home can be left unprepared for assuming these duties, especially if there will be limited communication between the parents during the deployment period. If the family recently moved before the deployment, the spouse at home might also still be looking for employment. In addition, families may face increased child-care costs that weren't necessary when two parents were at home. This can create an economic and sometimes unexpected burden on military families, and further stress for the child in your class.

Relocating During a Deployment: When one parent is deployed, the other parent sometimes takes the children and moves in with family members or others who are able to provide support during this difficult time—even if it means moving across the country. While such a decision might provide more adults to care for children, it can also add another disruption in the children's schooling and force them to adjust to another home and social environment. You may see some students leave your school for several months because their parent has deployed and the family has moved, or you may have new students enroll temporarily until their parent returns from deployment. These students may be especially anxious and vulnerable and may require special attention.

Multiple Deployments: One consequence of the fact that the wars in Iraq and Afghanistan have lasted so long is that many families have experienced multiple deployments. Just when a child gets used to having a parent home again, he or she is sent on another mission, and the relief associated with having a parent back in the home is not really experienced. "Multiple deployments" can also mean that a child has two parents in the military and both are deployed, or have back-to-back deployments. In this case, the child never has a stable home environment. One recent study, however, showed that some adolescents learn to cope better with each deployment. These students could possibly provide support and become role models for other students from military families.

Extended Deployments: Sometimes a deployment can last longer than expected, which can create extreme disappointment and anger in a family that is preparing to welcome home a service member at a specific time.

Well-Being of the Parent at Home: Studies have shown that one of the strongest predictors of emotional and behavioral problems for children during a deployment is how well the parent remaining with the child handles the stress that comes with being a military spouse. In addition, parents who use the support services available to them are more likely to have children that make it through the experience without significant negative outcomes.

Reintegration and Changing Relationships with the Deployed Parent: For younger and older children alike, a year or 18 months is a large period of time and one in which significant physical, social, and emotional development occurs. The way in which the child and the deployed parent interact, communicate, and play together may be significantly different following the deployment period. Expectations for both the child and the parent may be unrealistic. The deployment may also cause negative changes in the relationship between the parents, which could turn what the child expected to be a happy reunion into a different one, filled with fear, anxiety, and resentment.

CLASSROOM STRATEGIES

Here are suggestions for how teachers can support children with deployed parents in the classroom. Once again, the need to use multiple strategies would depend on the number of military students in your classroom and the number of them that have parents who are deployed.

Staying Informed: Ask parents to let you know when a deployment is scheduled or when a deployed parent is due to return. Staying aware of these significant events in a child's life can help you understand any changes the child is experiencing in the classroom and can allow you time to plan for adjustments in scheduling assignments or tests.

Attendance, Again: With the changes occurring at home, school may be the most stable place in a child's life. While it's obvious that the child will want to be home on the day that his or her parent leaves for a deployment, regular attendance maintains a sense of predictability for the child. Watch for repeated absences or increased tardiness following a deployment. Perhaps the parent who got the child ready in the morning or drove the child to school is the one that is deployed and the transfer of those duties to the other parent or another adult is not going well. Incentives for regular attendance or "bell-ringer" activities held at the beginning of the day can make the child want to be in the classroom. In addition, don't think that absences during the early grades are harmless. Even in preschool, regular attendance

The following teaching ideas come from the North Carolina Department of Public Instruction as part of the "NC Supports Military Children" section of its website. Many are geared toward elementary-age children, but could be adapted for older students.

- Encourage younger children to bring in some of the deployed parent's worn clothing and uniform items to use for dress-up play.
- Put together a "Proud to Be a Military Kid" bulletin board and encourage students to display pictures of military family members.
- Have a clock in the classroom that shows military time. A child with a deployed parent might want to help the class learn how to tell time the way their mother or father does.
- Arrange a field trip to a nearby military base or training facility.
- Write cards or letters to the deployed family member.
- Track the deployed parent's journey on a map, allowing the class to learn about the world.
- Turn a shoe box into a deployment time capsule. Fill the box with items like a piece of string as long as the child's height, a tracing of the child's hand or foot, a list of the child's favorites (song, television show, toy, etc.). Open them when the deployed parent returns to measure changes that have occurred.

establishes patterns that are important for children to carry throughout their school years.

Using Organizational Tools: A child with a deployed parent may be frequently distracted and disorganized. A student that used to turn in homework on time may now start missing assignments or losing them. Again, the parent who monitored homework completion or bought materials for out-of-class projects may be the one who is deployed. Use student planners or other organizational tools to help the student keep track of assignments. Give the child the option of completing homework at school to lessen the chances that it will not get turned in.

Increasing Communication with Parents: Be available to parents through phone and e-mail—not just at regular teacher-parent conference times. At the start of a deployment, encourage them to contact you to discuss how their child is handling the deployment and how it might be affecting his or her attitudes toward schoolwork. Keep the lines of communication open.

Geography Lesson: Provide a lesson on the regions of the world where military parents have been deployed or read literature set in those countries to provide students a glimpse into the culture of the country where the parent is serving.

Comments from Nonmilitary Students: Children are curious. Depending on their age, some may also have strong opinions about U.S. foreign policy that they want to share in your classroom. Answer their questions about war or other military missions to the best of your ability if the time is appropriate, without inserting your own opinions. But also frequently reiterate that the military parents of your students are brave men and women who are serving their country.

Adjusting Pacing by Focusing on Essential Content: If students with deployed parents appear overwhelmed and not able to keep up with their work because of what is happening at home, scale back the pace of your teaching to focus on the most critical standards for students to learn. A slower pace might be especially necessary when a deployment is beginning or when troops are returning.

Service Learning: Just as military parents are serving their country, students can learn to serve their community through integrated projects that combine academic skills with meeting local needs. Ask for input from military students or community organizations in picking appropriate projects, such as sending letters or care packages to military members who are deployed. An Oceanside, California, student who was named a Military Child of the Year in 2011, for example, started a program in which baby showers are planned for military wives whose husbands are deployed. Such activities can also build students' confidence, sense of independence, and self-worth.

Class Website: If you don't have a class website or Facebook page, consider creating one so deployed parents can stay informed on what their children are learning. You can post photos or videos of student projects, performances, or special field trips.

Support During Testing: If a unit is about to be deployed, or is about to return, avoid scheduling tests around those times. If testing dates are not flexible, make sure students and parents know well in advance when the test will be held. Plan extra review time or organize study groups to keep students focused on preparing for the test. Tell them you understand that they feel torn between their families and their schoolwork. Think about creating incentives, such as class parties, to encourage students to attend the day of the test.

Support for the Parents: Think of ways to reduce the burdens on parents remaining at home with the child. Limit long-term projects that require a lot of materials or work at home, or consider breaking long-term assignments into chunks and have interim deadlines to allow several opportunities for teacher feedback. Assign homework as a "packet" that can be completed over the course of the week instead of every night.

Counting on Parent Volunteers: If you have room parents, or if your school has a committee that helps families in need, ask them to organize rides to after-school activities, sports, play dates, "mother's day-out" arrangements, or study sessions for children with deployed parents. It's important that students stay involved in what they enjoy, but it's likely that the parent at home may feel overwhelmed and can't do it all alone.

"No Homework" Passes: Give students in your class a chance to earn these—possibly by doing extra credit work or through good behavior. They can be redeemed during block leave periods or when a parent is leaving or returning from a deployment.

Monitoring Nutrition: Watch for changes in a child's diet. If the student starts coming to school without having had breakfast or has stopped bringing a lunch to school, this could indicate increased stress on the parent or other caregivers in the home. Make sure the parents are informed about how to apply for the free or reduced-price lunch program if cost is the reason students are missing meals.

Responding to Emotional Outbursts: It's hard to predict what might trigger crying, yelling, or even aggression in a child who misses a parent. Explain to other students that strong displays of emotion from the child are normal. Help them find ways to constructively express their emotions without hurting others—perhaps through journal writing, artwork, or taking a break in the hallway. Especially with younger students, incorporate age-appropriate stories or activities that discuss negative emotions and how to manage them. The "Voices Reading" curriculum, for example, seeks to build academic and literacy skills through multicultural literature that supports social, emotional, and character development.

Making Students Feel Needed: A child may sometimes feel ignored when his or her parents are preparing for and coping with a deployment. Find special tasks or activities that students can take responsibility for in order to build their confidence, sense of independence, and self-worth.

Not Making Assumptions: Don't expect that you know how the child is feeling or reacting to a parent's deployment. While many may be upset, others may actually feel relieved when a parent leaves, depending on the particular child's family dynamics. Maybe there is less stress or tension in the home when the military parent is deployed. If this might be the case, the child may need greater attention from counselors or other support personnel after the parent returns.

RESEARCH HIGHLIGHTS ON PARENTAL DEPLOYMENT

- Studies show that since the beginning of the Iraq war, the demand for psychiatric services by military children has doubled to two million mental health outpatient visits (Gorman, Eide, & Hisle-Gorman, 2010). Psychiatric hospitalizations of military children for severe problems, including suicidal behaviors, have increased by 50%.
- A study by the RAND Corporation—involving 1,500 children who attended a summer camp program offered by the National Military Family Association—found that longer periods of deployment are associated with more social and emotional problems for children (Richardson et al., 2011). The effects of deployment also vary by children's age and gender. Older, rather than younger, students were more likely to have problems in school and with their peers during deployment. Girls were more likely than boys to have problems related to their parent returning from duty.
- Children as young as 3 can experience emotional and behavioral issues related to a parent's deployment, according to a 2008 study by Molinda M. Chartrand from the Boston University School of Public Health. This finding has implications for elementary schools and those that operate preschool or other early-childhood programs. When compared to children without deployed parents, preschoolers with a parent deployed during wartime had higher rates of internalizing behaviors, such as anxiety, depression, and withdrawal, and externalizing behaviors, such as attention difficulties and aggression.
- Alyssa J. Mansfield, formerly of the University of North Carolina at Chapel Hill and now with the National Center for Posttraumatic Stress Disorder in Honolulu, found that children with a parent who was deployed in Operation Iraqi Freedom and Operation Enduring Freedom for longer periods were more likely to receive a diagnosis of a mental health problem than children whose parents did not deploy (Mansfield et al., 2011). The study included 307,520 children, of whom 16.7% had a mental health diagnosis. More than 62% of parents were deployed at least once during the period, for an average of 11 months. The study found that mental health problems were more likely among children who had a parent deployed at least once to Iraq or Afghanistan. The likelihood of a mental health diagnosis increased

with longer deployments. Among the 6,579 mental health diagnoses observed, the most common were acute stress reaction and adjustment disorders, depressive disorders, and behavioral disorders.

RESOURCES

Listed below are organizations, programs, and publications that can increase a teacher's understanding of the issues military families face when a parent is deployed.

Educator's Guide to the Military Child During Deployment: This document was sponsored by the Educational Opportunities Directorate of the Department of Defense in collaboration with Marleen Wong, a co-principal investigator of Building Capacity. http://one.center-school.org/search-document-detail.php?ID=1019

Military-Connected Students and Public School Attendance Policies: This report from the Military Child Education Coalition provides an informative section on the ways some states handle attendance issues related to block leave or other events related to deployment. http://www.militarychild.org/public/upload/files/SchoolAttendancePoliciesFINAL.pdf

Military Deployment and Families: This audio is part of the Healthy Children initiative of the American Academy of Pediatrics. http://www.healthychildren.org/English/family-life/family-dynamics/pages/Military-Deployment-and-Families.aspx

Young Children on the Homefront: Family Stories, Family Strengths: This DVD is useful to teachers who work with young children. Part of the Zero to Three organization's Coming Together Around Military Families initiative, the DVD provides tips and strategies for supporting children before, during, and after a deployment. Themes include Staying Connected, Stress and Behavior, Routines and Reunification. http://www.zerotothree.org/about-us/funded-projects/military-families/children-on-the-homefront.html. Zero to Three also provides other tools appropriate for young children. "More Changes? Are You Kidding Me?" is a short two-page flier about reintegration. And *Home Again* is a board book for young children, parents, and caregivers about the reunification experience.

Ready, Set, Go!: This manual and training opportunity is part of Operation: Military Kids, the U.S. Army's effort to partner with community organizations to support military families during deployment. A wide variety of other resources and links are also available at this site. http://www.4-hmilitarypartnerships.org/DesktopDefault.aspx?tabid=127

Surviving Deployment.com: This site provides ideas for activities, links to other resources, and helpful articles, such as "Helping Children Handle Deployments." It is written for parents, but useful for teachers as well. http://www.survivingdeployment.com/articles.html

Deployment Kids.com: A website for kids that is all theirs, but can also give teachers some ideas for fun activities. http://www.deploymentkids.com/

How to Prepare Our Children and Stay Involved in Their Education During Deployment: This booklet from the Military Child Education Coalition offers suggestions for both parents and educators and provides insight into some of the thoughts and feelings that students might have surrounding the deployment of a parent. http://www.militarychild.org/files/pdfs/DeploymentBooklet.pdf

Helping Children Cope with the Challenges of War and Terrorism: This workbook provides activities for adults and children to identify, understand, and cope with their feelings. http://www.7-dippity.com/other/UWA_war_book.pdf

Talk, Listen, Connect: This is an initiative of Sesame Workshop, the organization behind *Sesame Street.* In partnership with Walmart and The New York Office of Mental Health, the effort focuses on helping young children of military members cope with feelings, challenges, and concerns related to deployment. The site offers videos featuring popular Muppet characters as well as other materials. http://www.sesameworkshop.org/what-we-do/our-work/reaching-out-to-military-families-6-detail.html

Helping Children Cope When a Loved One Is on Deployment: This article from the National Association for the Education of Young Children can specifically help preschool and primary grade teachers respond to children's questions, understand their emotional reactions, and provide support in the classroom. http://www.naeyc.org/files/yc/file/200701/BTJAllen.pdf

4. Deployment

CHAPTER 5

Traumatic Experiences

> We're used to working with specific support systems that are in place for families within specific bases, so we'll call up a base and say "What's your family support program? Can we refer a child to it?" But the new norm is we need to take ownership of it at schools. We can't assume that kids are going to be ready to learn just because we're putting a piece of paper in front of them that talks about math. We have to consider what's happening outside of school and what the stressors are and how that impacts learning.
>
> —Kimberly Israel, Pupil Services Project Specialist,
> Escondido Union School District

Over the course of your career as a teacher, you will encounter a range of situations in which painful experiences affecting your students have an impact on your classroom. These can be as temporary as a kindergartner's skinned knee on the playground or as life-changing as a divorce, a serious illness, or even a parent's death.

Teachers know that children's physical, mental, and emotional well-being often determines how well they do in school. But they may have differing views on their role in helping students through the troubling—and even traumatic—events in their lives.

Some may feel their role is only to teach the curriculum and focus on making sure children acquire the knowledge and skills they need for the next grade. Family tragedies or a child's personal problems should be tended to only by outside counselors, faith-based organizations, or other trained professionals—it's not the school's job.

Others may agree their mission is to teach the curriculum, but also see schools as communities in which children's nonacademic needs can be addressed by counselors, nurses, psychologists, and other support personnel who are trained to treat physical, mental, and emotional issues.

Lastly, some teachers may feel it is appropriate to create a sense of community and caring within the classroom, and think that children should learn to support each other and show compassion when a classmate is having a hard time. They may believe it is their responsibility to nurture students' academic growth, but also to respond when factors outside the classroom affect a child's performance.

Whichever of these three categories you are in will determine your approach to many of the issues affecting military students—which can include exposure to uncomfortable topics and frightening situations and events that civilian children typically don't have to worry about.

If you count yourself among those educators in the first or second categories, realize that the issues children face outside of school will still affect how they function in your classroom. If you consider yourself among those teachers in the third category, you may still need support and professional development in how to:

- recognize the signs that children are struggling
- support social-emotional development in the classroom
- build a sense of community among your students

MILITARY CHILDREN AND TRAUMA

As mentioned in Chapter 4, simply being separated from a parent for an extended period can be more upsetting for some children than it is for others,

How Will You Know If a Child Needs Help from a Mental Health Professional?

These signs to watch for come from *Life & Loss: A Guide to Help Grieving Children* by Linda Goldman, 2000. It is normal for children to exhibit some of these behaviors, she writes. But it is the "extreme behaviors and intensity of feelings and actions" that indicate a need for help.

- Child continually refuses to share thoughts or feelings about loss
- Child is extremely clingy to adults
- Child has been lied to about loss
- Child threatens to hurt him or herself
- Child won't socialize
- Child becomes involved in drugs or alcohol
- Child is cruel to animals or physically abusive to other children
- Child has had a very difficult relationship with a parent or loved one who has died
- Child shows extremes in not sleeping or eating
- Child is failing school
- Child exhibits sudden unexplained change

5. Traumatic Experiences

depending on a variety of factors. For some military children, one more school transfer—especially if previous moves were problematic—may be the event that sparks emotions and behavior that are more serious than just being disappointed and angry.

Living with fear that a parent—or another relative—serving in the military is in danger can traumatize a child to the point where it significantly affects his or her ability to function in the school environment.

In addition, members of the military often return from a wartime deployment changed by the experience. The effects can be physical—as with an injury—or psychological. But either way, they can impact a service member's parenting ability.

As a classroom teacher, you should be prepared for these possibilities, aware of military and community resources available to returning veterans and their families, and equipped with strategies that can support children coping with trauma.

Your school can be a refuge and a welcome distraction for military families if you and others in your school are prepared in advance to respond to these issues and recognize that you can play a part in helping the child survive the trauma.

WOUNDED PARENTS

Many thousands of children have had a parent wounded in action since the beginning of the wars in Iraq and Afghanistan.

Some injuries are serious enough to require rehabilitation and could extend the time that a child is separated from his or her parent. A debilitating injury can dramatically affect that parent's relationship with the child and can continue to create shifting responsibilities in the home, even though the deployed parent has returned.

But sometimes the damage is invisible, as is the case with traumatic brain injury (TBI), a condition in which a violent blow to the head causes a collision between the brain and the inside of the skull. The rampant use of improvised explosive devices (IEDs) by enemy forces in Iraq and Afghanistan has resulted in many veterans returning with TBI, which is hard to diagnose, but can have lasting effects.

To a child, especially a young child, his or her parent may appear the same. But the symptoms, such as headaches, concentration problems, mood changes, depression, anxiety, and fatigue can significantly interfere with family relationships.

Even if a parent returns from battle without a physical injury, many suffer from psychological wounds that increase stress in the home, damage the relationship between the parent and the child, and can further affect how that child is performing in your school. Depression, suicidal thoughts, post-traumatic stress disorder (PTSD), substance abuse, and other mental health issues are not uncommon among returning veterans.

Children, as a result, can suffer just as much as their parents. Parents with PTSD may avoid certain subjects or situations that are reminders of the violence or trauma they experienced. They may constantly appear on edge or about to explode with anger, and even re-experience traumatic events as if they were still on the battlefield.

All of these behaviors are upsetting for children and affect their relationship with their parent. They may feel that they are the cause of reminding their parent of the trauma. They might feel as if their parent doesn't love them, and they too may begin to exhibit symptoms similar to those of their parent. Some experts describe the effects of trauma on the soldiers' spouses and children as "secondary traumatization."

Some studies have also shown that child maltreatment—including physical, emotional, or sexual abuse—increased among military families as more troops were being sent into Iraq and Afghanistan.

Don't assume that because a military parent has been deployed or was injured in combat that he or she is going to become violent, suicidal, or display other symptoms of serious mental illness. But war wounds—both physical and psychological—can help to explain changes in a student's behavior at school.

THE DEATH OF A PARENT

A death in the family of one of your students affects not only the student, but also your entire class. Because the military has specific procedures for notifying and caring for family members when a service member dies, classroom teachers may not be among the first to know if the parent of a child in their classroom has died in combat or as a result of another military action.

That's one reason why it is essential for schools to have a plan in place for responding to a parent's death—whether the parent is in the military or not.

In the event of a parent's death, the way a teacher responds is not only significant for the child who has lost a parent, but will also serve as an example to the rest of the students in the class, many of whom will be struggling with how to talk to the student and be supportive of them when he or she returns to your classroom.

Often, when someone's relative dies, the people around them don't say anything because they don't want to offend anyone, they are afraid of saying the wrong thing or triggering an emotional reaction, or they don't want to appear intrusive. But children spend so much of their lives in school that pretending nothing has happened is unrealistic and the silence could hinder how that child learns to adapt to his or her loss.

MAJOR ISSUES RELATED TO TRAUMA

Military families often face complex and complicated issues when coping with the aftermath of war, many of which can seriously distract children from their responsibilities at school and impact their success in the classroom. The following are topics that you should be prepared to address.

Special Education Referrals: Children often do not have the words to explain why are they are acting out, having tantrums, or not concentrating in class. Maybe their parents argue at home, they are worried about whether their parents have enough money, or a parent came back from Iraq in a wheelchair. They may not even understand the range of emotions they are feeling. Behavioral, emotional, and learning problems, however, are often considered reasons to refer a child for special education, especially if teachers don't know that the child's difficulties are related to being in a military family. See our expanded section on special education in Chapter 2.

Effects on the Other Parent: If a military parent returns from battle with a serious injury, the other parent may be so traumatized by that experience—or busy with the person's treatment and recovery—that he or she cannot give appropriate care and attention to the child. The same could be the case with PTSD or other mental health problems. Furthermore, if one parent has died, the surviving parent may not be able to carry on with routines that allow the child to do well in school.

Another Move: If a parent is injured, the family may be faced with relocating again in order for that parent to receive appropriate medical care or rehabilitation. If a military parent dies, this could also precipitate another move so the surviving parent can be closer to friends and extended family members. This creates another community and school transition for the child that was not expected in the normal course of being part of a military family. If your school is located near a large military medical facility, you may have students in your class who are there temporarily while an injured parent is being treated. These students also may present unique challenges in your class.

Loss of Military Identity: Even when military children attend regular public schools, they have grown up in a military community and lifestyle

Trauma-sensitive schools acknowledge the prevalence of traumatic occurrence in students' lives and create a flexible framework that provides universal supports, is sensitive to unique needs of students, and is mindful of avoiding re-traumatization.

—From "Creating Trauma-Sensitive Schools," a PowerPoint presentation from the Wisconsin Department of Public Instruction

The presentation is available at: http://www.dpi.wi.gov/sspw/mhtrauma.html

that is part of how they identify themselves. Their close friends are probably other military children, and they perhaps attend recreation or summer programs especially designed for children of military members. If a parent doesn't return to active duty following an injury, or if a military parent dies, a child's lifestyle and routine could change abruptly. This is another level of loss and transition for a military child.

Perceptions of the Military Parent: If the school community views the military member as a hero and as someone who has performed a valuable service to the country, the child will share in that sense of pride and appreciation. But if a death or injury was self-inflicted—or if substance abuse was involved—the community is likely to treat the family differently and the child may feel shame.

Disengagement in Schoolwork: If a parent is seriously injured, has died, or is experiencing significant trauma following reintegration, a child may feel that everything else in life is insignificant compared to the issues being confronted at home. Telling a child to focus on schoolwork may only generate resentment and make him or her think that you don't care. Furthermore, the child may be reluctant to attend school in hopes of avoiding questions about what is happening at home.

CLASSROOM STRATEGIES

Below are suggestions for creating a classroom environment that is sensitive to military students experiencing grief or trauma.

Putting Events in Context: Current wars can create multiple opportunities for students to explore past wars, to study the political, religious, and cultural factors that led to various conflicts, and to gain a better

5. Traumatic Experiences

understanding of history. Just because children are from military families doesn't mean they have accurate information about the military's objectives. Creating timelines, journaling, and other assignments can be used to connect classroom learning with world events. They can also serve as an outlet for students to express thoughts or raise questions they don't feel comfortable discussing.

Maintaining Routine: If a student's parent has died or been seriously injured, allow time for discussion and answering questions, providing the facts that you know, but then return to your normal classroom routine as soon as possible to give the student—and all students in your class—a sense of security and stability.

Posting a Daily Schedule: Children experiencing trauma at home may feel helpless and on edge because they never know what to expect. Surprises at school, such as a classroom visitor or a special assembly, may only contribute to their stress. A daily schedule can reinforce the idea of the classroom as a stable place where children know what is going to happen next.

Alternative Assignments: Just as places, events, or sensations may trigger disturbing reminders of war for a military parent, comments made in your classroom or even topics you may be teaching about may elicit upsetting thoughts for military children—enough that they can't complete their work. Consider allowing a student to choose an alternate topic for a report or project if that is more comforting, but also explain that you need to stick to the curriculum and that you—or another adult—can help the student through his or her fears and emotions.

Classroom Displays: A bulletin board, banner, or other display honoring members of the military that previously made a child feel welcomed and appreciated may now only serve as a disturbing reminder of what their parent and the rest of their family has been through. Discuss with the child whether it should be removed or replaced with something else.

Planting a Garden: School gardens are used for a variety of curricular purposes—to teach science, to encourage students to eat healthier, and to develop a sense of responsibility. Planting flowers or trees can also serve as a way to honor members of the military who have died, as well as other heroes from the community.

Allowing Breaks: While routine is good, students experiencing extreme stress or trauma may also need opportunities to excuse themselves from class during the school day to speak to a counselor or social worker, or to block out conversations or topics that are reminding them of upsetting events at home.

Online Learning: If a child is missing–or avoiding–school because of a parent's injury, death, or other trauma in the home, are there ways that the student can satisfy assignments using a home computer?

Honoring the Family: If a military parent has died, you and your class may or may not be able to attend the funeral–depending on the wishes of the family. But you and your students can arrange a separate memorial for the parent if your school hasn't already planned something. Class activities can also include making cards or writing letters to show support for the family. Such activities, however, should be done in consultation with the family and only when the child is ready.

Encouraging the Child to Talk to an Adult: Even if a child is not displaying emotional difficulty in your class, remind him or her that a counselor or another adult in the school is available to talk with about what is happening at home. A child–especially an adolescent–who initially tries to be strong for other members of the family in a crisis might later experience depression or other feelings of being overwhelmed by the burden.

Preparing for Separation Problems: If a child has had one parent die, he or she may have a particularly hard time separating from the other parent to come to school. This may especially be the case among younger students. Consider ways to ease the child's transition to school each day, perhaps by giving the child a break or two during the day to call his or her parent on the phone or allowing him or her to bring something in their backpack that provides comfort.

Daily Report Cards: This strategy is sometimes used with students who have a hard time getting through the school day and focusing on their assignments. Such an approach could also be customized for a child that has experienced significant trauma and is having difficulty completing assignments, getting along with peers, or following school rules. This process may become a new routine for the child that assists in setting goals and working through strong emotions.

Staying Involved: It is not unusual for a student who has been through a traumatic event to withdraw from social situations or give up activities he or she used to enjoy. He or she might feel that he doesn't deserve to have a good time because someone at home is suffering, or he or she might want to avoid situations in which someone is always asking about how things are going. But watch for signs that he or she is avoiding all extracurriculars or other opportunities to socialize completely. These can serve as an outlet for recovery and feeling normal again.

Replacing Negative Thoughts: This strategy comes from the Support for Students Exposed to Trauma (SSET) program—a support group curriculum developed by researchers at RAND in collaboration with Marleen Wong, an Assistant Dean in the USC School of Social Work and a co-principal investigator for Building Capacity. A child experiencing trauma may frequently express negative thoughts out of fear that the event or situation will happen again. This might apply to a child who is worried about his or her parents' reaction to a poor test grade, as in the example shown in the box, or one who is facing a parent's symptoms of PTSD at home. Help the student challenge negative thinking by coming up with alternative, more positive thoughts.

Contacting the Next School: This type of contact is the least likely to occur at the high school level because teachers only have the student for one period and everyone might think that someone else in the school will take responsibility for this task. But if another move is imminent, administrators or counselors at the child's school should be made aware if the child has been dealing with experiences that can drastically affect their progress in school and their future beyond graduation.

Finding Meaning: It's normal for children to think only about how a tragedy, a parent's illness, or some other challenging situation affects them

---

Example of a Negative Thought:

- "I'm going to get a bad grade on my report card in math."

Examples of Helpful Thoughts:

- "I've done well on other tests."
- "Everyone did badly on this test."
- "I can study more next time."
- "I can ask the teacher if I can earn extra credit to make up for the grade."
- "I can see about getting a tutor."

Support for Students Exposed to Trauma: The SSET Program,
Lisa H. Jaycox, Audra K. Langley, Kristin L. Dean

and their normal routine. But some children also live through such events to help others or to raise awareness about a particular need. Help children understand that they are not alone, that there are organizations of military children who have been through similar circumstances, and that they too can provide strength and understanding for others facing difficult times.

Not Forgetting the Other Students: A crisis in the life of one student can often affect those around him or her. Even if it just appears that other students are acting out or appearing sad because they too want extra attention, be aware that a tragedy can leave other students feeling scared or insecure.

RESOURCES

The following resources and organizations provide teachers with advice and information on handling issues of grief and trauma. While some are focused specifically on military children, others are more general.

The National Child Traumatic Stress Network: This site explains types of trauma and provides a section focusing specifically on military children and families as well as a section geared toward educators. http://www. nctsnet.org/

Talk, Listen, Connect: This is an initiative of Sesame Workshop, the organization behind *Sesame Street*. In partnership with Walmart, and The New York Office of Mental Health, the effort includes videos and other materials focused on helping young children of military members cope with grief. http://www.sesameworkshop.org/what-we-do/our-work/reaching-out-to-military-families-6-detail.html

Child's Grief Education Association: This organization's website includes a section on military families in addition to useful basic advice on helping children deal with grief and loss. http://www.childgrief.org/childgrief.htm

Helping Children Cope with Loss, Death, and Grief: Tips for Teachers and Parents: This article from the National Association of School Psychologists provides advice to teachers on how to handle the issues of death and grief in the classroom. http://nasponline.org/resources/crisis_safety/griefwar.pdf

Tragedy Assistance Program for Survivors: This organization provides around-the-clock services for military families, such as emotional support, crisis intervention, grief and trauma resources and "Good Grief" camps for children. http://www.taps.org/

When Death Impacts Your School: This article from The Dougy Center: The National Center for Grieving Children and Families gives teachers specific suggestions on how to communicate with grieving students in the classroom, including what and what not to say. http://www.dougy.org/grief-resources/death-impacts-your-school/

National Military Family Association: This organization has a section on its website focusing on wounded warriors. It is meant for military families but can be informative for educators. Click on the "Your Benefits" tab. http://www.militaryfamily.org/

When a Child's Parent Has PTSD: The National Center for PTSD at the U.S. Department of Veterans Affairs provides useful information on how a parent's PTSD can affect their child. http://www.ptsd.va.gov/public/pages/children-of-vets-adults-ptsd.asp

The National Institute for Trauma and Loss in Children provides direct services to traumatized children and families as well as resource materials to help children. The website has a series of podcasts featuring professionals who have worked with military families regarding deployment and other experiences. http://www.starrtraining.org/tlc

Trauma Faced by Children of Military Families: What Every Policymaker Should Know is available on the National Center for Children in Poverty website. It provides a simple overview of the demographics of military children, many of the challenges they face, key research findings related to deployment and mental health, as well as some of the resources designed to help military families. http://www.nccp.org/publications/pub_938.html

"Children of Wounded Warriors: Guidance for Caregivers": This article from eXtension—which presents research and knowledge from land-grant universities across the United States—suggests ways to help children prepare for and adjust to a parent's serious injury. While it is intended for parents, it can also be helpful to teachers and child-care providers. http://www.extension.org/pages/60148/children-of-wounded-warriors:-guidance-for-caregivers

Support for Students Exposed to Trauma: The SSET Program: Developed by researchers at RAND in collaboration with Marleen Wong of USC, this manual is designed to be used by teachers and provides lesson plans, materials, and worksheets for use in a group setting. The program was not originally intended for military children, but can apply to many of the situations they might be facing. http://www.rand.org/pubs/research_briefs/RB9443-1/index1.html

Listen, Protect, Connect—Model and Teach: Psychological First Aid (PFA) for Students and Teachers: This booklet from the National Center for School Crisis and Bereavement is primarily intended to focus on supporting students after disasters or similar emergencies, but it provides some good suggestions for teachers who may have students that are struggling in school following a traumatic event. http://www.cincinnatichildrens.org/assets/0/78/1067/4357/4389/17e1ee0b-ede2-4abc-ac8c-192ec193101d.pdf

---

Promising Practice Spotlight: Heroes' Tree

The Heroes' Tree is one practice that a school can use to honor both living and deceased members of the military. The community recognizes and honors both current and past members of the Armed Forces. Founded by authors Stephanie Pickup and Marlene Lee, the project is a partnership led by the Military Family Research Institute (MFRI) at Purdue University.

Heroes' Trees are similar to Christmas trees, but are adorned with handmade ornaments featuring photographs of military service members or drawings that represent service members. While the trees have been placed in local libraries in Indiana, schools are also appropriate places for the trees—allowing students to pay tribute to heroes in their lives and to learn about the role of the military in U.S. history.

Example of a Heroes' Tree ornament

The project is noncontroversial and all-inclusive, explains Kathy Broniarczyk, the director of outreach for MFRI, because the servicemen and women honored don't have to be current members of the military. They can be someone's grandfather or uncle or a long-deceased

---

5. Traumatic Experiences

relative who served in a past war. The project raises awareness of the sacrifices that have been made by service members and their families and creates opportunities for a variety of learning experiences for students.

In addition to the literal trees placed in libraries and other places where members of the community gather, a Virtual Heroes' Tree has also been created to serve as a web-based extension of the project, allowing anyone to take part in viewing information on the members being honored and to learn about their service.

In its resource guide, the MFRI has also compiled an extensive list of ideas for school and community programs involving children and youth. Many would be appropriate for school service-learning projects. They include:

- Taking a graveyard exploration and writing down information from a tombstone of a deceased veteran
- Using library genealogy resources to investigate and collect biographical information on living local relatives of the veteran, and then interviewing the relatives to learn more about the service member's military experience
- Creating family trees that make note of any relatives who served in the Armed Forces or in military branches of other countries
- Identifying the needs of veterans in local nursing homes and Veterans' Administration hospitals and brainstorming ideas for helping them
- Interviewing veterans about their military service, any memorable stories, their job in the military, and whether they served during a war

To access the resource guide, view the Virtual Heroes' Tree and learn more about the Heroes' Tree program, visit: http://www.cfs.purdue.edu/mfri/public/oht/Default.aspx

CHAPTER 6

Using Data to Improve School Climate for Military Students

The teaching profession has changed over the past decades to include a much greater emphasis on using data to better understand and meet students' needs in the classroom.

Frequent assessments can tell you whether students have grasped what you are teaching and which students might need additional—or a different type of—instruction. In many schools, students are encouraged to track their own progress so they can understand where they need extra practice.

Collecting information on nonacademic issues can also help schools identify strengths and weaknesses among students and point to the factors that help students be successful in school as well as those that create obstacles to learning.

SCHOOL SAFETY AND CLIMATE SURVEYS

The environment in which students go to school every day has been found to have an effect on how they learn. A student who feels that the adults in the school care about him is more likely to feel positive about learning than a student who doesn't feel supported. Students who are experimenting with drugs or alcohol are likely to begin having trouble academically. And those who are afraid of being teased or hurt by a bully are going to have a harder time concentrating on schoolwork.

To better understand these factors, many school districts use anonymous surveys to collect information on school climate and the risk and resiliency factors that are part of students' lives. These surveys can help to identify which groups of students are having more difficulty coping with the challenges of social relationships, feel pressured by peers to try drugs or alcohol, or have concerns about their safety.

Your students' parents and you as a teacher might also have an opportunity to fill out a companion survey that gathers multiple perspectives on the same topics.

It is common for the results of these surveys to show outcomes by subgroups, such as by gender, race, and ethnicity, or grade level. If you have students from military families in your school or classroom, however, you might also want to know how their experiences and opinions compare to those of other students in the school. For the most part, many of these students' needs have been left unidentified. Or teachers have made assumptions about these students based on stereotypes.

But states are now beginning to add questions on these surveys specifically for military students since these children have unique family circumstances and might have needs that are not typical among nonmilitary students.

"NO MORE DATA, PLEASE!"

Your first reaction at the thought of administering or completing a survey like this in your classroom might be one of exasperation. Why should you devote class time to giving a survey when no one is going to do anything with the results? You might also think you already know your students well enough to know who is getting into trouble, who feels sad too often, and who is achieving in spite of having a troubled home life.

You most likely would not be the only teacher in your school that has grown skeptical and even cynical toward anything that has to do with data collection or research. Your questions may include:

- Why is the data being collected?
- How will it be used?
- Will it reflect badly on my school, my classroom, or me?

In addition, outside researchers often gain access to schools, conduct studies and interviews and then generate reports that are either never available or are not relevant to you, your students, or their parents.

A DEMOCRATIC PROCESS

These surveys, however, are a chance for you and your students to tell school leaders and policymakers about the problems or positive attributes of your school. Some students who will never approach you to share their experiences will feel more comfortable expressing themselves in an anonymous survey. The results of these surveys are sometimes used to make decisions regarding school funding, staff distribution or certain intervention programs. Providing honest and thoughtful answers—and encouraging your students to do the same—allows you to take an active part in that process.

For example, your school district might be implementing Positive Behavioral Interventions and Support, but might only be able to afford to train teachers in a subset of schools. Surveys might be used to identify whether your school should be involved. These surveys can also assist your school in implementing Response to Intervention, a method designed to better identify which students are more likely to have trouble learning.

Ask your principal to make sure the results are made available so that teachers and other staff members can discuss the findings and provide input on which issues require the most attention.

GETTING STUDENTS READY

Students may also not feel a need to take such a survey seriously. Or they may just randomly fill in the bubbles or check boxes without reading the questions carefully. Conducting some short practice surveys in your classroom—on topics that interest them—and sharing the results with them can help them see the value in participating in a survey. You might also make a change in your classroom, based on their opinions, to show how their input can make a difference.

Here's a concrete example of how some schools are involving students in improving something that matters a great deal to them—the lunch menu. Many schools have recruited students for tasting sessions so that officials can see what menu creations students respond well to and which ones they refuse to try. The students are involved in choosing what will be served in their schools before it is prepared for everyone. Similar efforts can be made on a variety of topics, and once students believe that school leaders are interested in what they have to say, they are more likely to be truthful and share their views on issues that matter to them.

You might want to take some similar steps with parents if they are going to be involved in the survey process. Send parents an e-mail to encourage them to fill out the surveys.

California's School Climate, Health, and Learning Survey, for example, gathers information from teachers, students, and parents on the risk and resiliency factors that affect students' success in school and life. In 2010, a "military module" was added to the survey system to provide a better picture of the issues and challenges military children are facing. The information gathered is used to identify students' needs and find appropriate services, programs, and activities to improve school experiences for students.

In the tables below, we provide examples of the topic areas and types of questions that appear in both the "core" survey and the military module. We include examples from the surveys given to students, school staff and parents.

Examples of Modules and Questions from the California Healthy Kids Survey (CHKS) for High School Students

Topics	Examples of Questions
Module A: Core	
1. Background Info	What is your gender?; Grade?
2. School Connectedness and Participation	I feel close to people at this school.
3. Adult Support and Participation in Community	Outside of my home and school, there is an adult who really cares about me.
4. Eating Habits	Did you eat breakfast today?
5. Alcohol, Tobacco, Marijuana, & Other Drug Use	During your *life*, how many times have you used or tried a whole cigarette?
6. Violence, Safety, Harassment & Bullying	During the *past 12 months*, how many times on school property have you been pushed, shoved, slapped, hit, or kicked by someone who wasn't just kidding around?
7. Sadness, Suicidal Thoughts	During the *past 12 months*, did you ever seriously consider attempting suicide?
8. Betting/ Gambling	During the *past 12 months*, how often have you bet/ gambled, even casually, for money or valuables in card or dice games (such as poker, blackjack, or craps)?
Military Module	
1. Military Connectedness	Who in your family is *currently* in the military?
2. Personal and Family Strengths	My family is very close and we support each other; I am more independent than many of my friends.
3. School Experiences	Other students in school do not really understand my family life; I have a hard time making friends because I have to change schools often.
4. Mood and Affect	In the *last 30 days*, how often did you feel full of energy?
5. Experiences as a Military Student	In the *last 5 years*, how many times did you change your school because your family had to move?

Additional Available Modules
Resilience Supplemental
AOD (Alcohol and Other Drugs), Violence, & Suicide
Tobacco
Physical Health & Nutrition
Sexual Behavior
District Afterschool (DASM)
Gang Risk Awareness
Service Learning
Closing the Achievement Gap (CTAG)
Safe and Supportive Schools (S3)
After-school Program
Building Healthy Communities (BHC)
School Health Center
California Student Survey (CSS)

Examples of Modules and Questions from the School Staff Survey (California School Climate Survey—CSCS)

Topics	Sample Questions
1. School Social and Academic Climate	This school is a supportive and inviting place for students to learn; is a supportive and inviting place for staff to work.
2. Discipline and Safety	Handles discipline problems fairly; is a safe place for students
3. Adult Support of Students	How many adults really care about every student?
4. Adult Mutual Support	How many adults support and treat each other with respect?
5. Need for Professional Development	Areas such as: meeting academic standards; evidence-based methods of instruction; serving English language learners
6. Perceptions of Students	How many students are motivated to learn; are well behaved?
7. Problems in School	How much of a problem at this school is student alcohol and drug use?; racial/ethnic conflict among students?
8. School Policies and Practices	This school promotes personnel participation in decisionmaking that affects school practices and policies; provides complete state-adopted instructional materials for students with IEPs.

Topics	Sample Questions
Military Module	
1. Military-Connected Students and Needs and Strengths	Many military students have additional educational needs; Military students have additional strengths due to their family circumstances.
2. School's Inclusion of Military-Connected Students	This school provides a welcoming environment to military students and their families; has additional services for students whose parents are deployed.
3. Need for Professional Development Related to Military-Connected Students	I need professional development in order to understand military culture; understand the effects of deployment cycles.
Additional Sections/Modules	
Staff who have responsibilities for services or instruction related to health, prevention, discipline, counseling, and/or safety	This school collaborates well with community organizations to help address substance use or other problems among youth; punishes first-time violations of alcohol or other drug policies by at least an out-of-school suspension.
	To what extent the school provides nutritional instruction?; alcohol or drug use prevention instruction?
School personnel with responsibilities for teaching or providing related services to students with individualized education programs (IEPs).	This school integrates special education into its daily operations; has a climate that encourages me to continue in my role of service to students with IEPs.

Examples of Modules and Questions from the California School Parent Survey

Topics	Sample Questions
1. Background	Does one or more of your children receive a free or reduced-price breakfast or lunch at this school?; In what grade is your child?
2. Perceptions of School	Promotes academic success for *all* students; gives my child opportunities to participate in classroom activities
3. School Problems	Student alcohol and drug use?; weapons possession?
4. School Policies and Practices	Actively seeks the input of parents before making important decisions; has a supportive learning environment for my child

Topics	Sample Questions
Military Module	
1. Background	How many times have you been deployed outside the United States?
2. Importance of School Factors	Academic reputation; convenience
3. Need for Additional Services	Additional tutoring; after-school activities
4. Satisfaction	The respect school staff show to military families?; The understanding teachers show you as a military parent?

MAKING POSITIVE CHANGES

Paper or online surveys are one tool for gathering information from members of the school community. Other methods, such as focus groups and mapping, might not produce quantitative data. But they are interactive, can provide perspectives that can't be captured on a survey, and can communicate to students, parents, and teachers that the school is interested in their opinions and concerns.

Mapping, for example, is used to identify locations within a school where problem behavior, such as bullying, fights, or drug and alcohol use, might be more likely to occur. It can also be used to pinpoint areas and times that make students feel safer and happier in school. This technique is intended to include all stakeholders—students, teachers, and other staff members—in providing their perspectives on where such spots are located in the school, at what times of day the behavior occurs, and who is present when it happens. An important part of the process is gathering each student's theory on why specific times and locations within the school are more prone to these situations, and then following up with solutions to alleviate the problem.

Schools that have used the mapping process to address issues of violence or bullying in their schools have found it to be highly effective. For example, one high school learned that fights were occurring among 11th and 12th graders right outside a gym and near the parking lot immediately after school. Students and teachers agreed that the visible presence of school staff should be increased in and around the parking lot for 20 minutes after school.

In another school, students reported during the mapping process that they felt unsafe near the school gate at the end of day. The information was relayed to the principal, who then observed the flow of "traffic" through the gate, making sure she was not noticed by the students. After a couple of

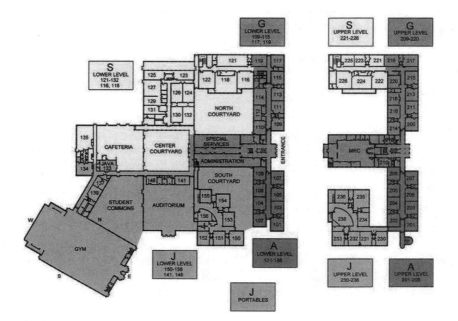

observations, she concluded that since only one gate was open, the clustering of students trying to exit the gate all at one time led to pushing, shoving, and skirmishes among impatient students. As a solution, she simply opened up another gate to ease the congestion. She further decided to assign teachers to greet the students as they were leaving school, making sure to call students by their names and express an interest in how their day went.

Another method for involving students in making improvements at their school is the *Student Listening Circle*, also known as the "fishbowl." This has been used to help schools understand data on student resiliency and youth development. In schools that use this approach, the adults have remained committed to implementing the changes suggested as a result of the process.

The listening circle is a special type of focus group that includes eight to 10 students who respond to five or six questions based on data from the survey on nonacademic barriers to learning. Roughly the same number of adults is chosen to listen to what the students have to say. Three simultaneous listening circles are often held as part of a forum. One focuses on the role of the family, another on the role of the school, and the third on the community.

In the schools that have used this strategy, tangible improvements have been made based on the feedback provided by the students. For example, in one school, students complained that they often had tests in more than

one subject on the same day. In response, a more manageable schedule was created to avoid those situations. In another school, students complained about the condition of the restrooms. So administrators made sure they were promptly cleaned and regularly stocked with toilet paper, paper towels, and soap. In a third school, a mentoring program was created involving not only teachers but other school staff members.

CONCLUSION

Schools and districts regularly collect information on a variety of achievement and other student indicators. But that's often where the process stops. School climate, safety, and health and behavior surveys can also provide valuable information that can be used to improve learning conditions for students. As a teacher, you can lobby school, district, and state officials to share the information with those involved and use it to make positive changes at the school level. You can also emphasize the importance of including issues that are of importance to military students and their families in surveys and focus group discussions. This will allow you to better understand the issues that concern them.

6. Using Data to
Improve Schools

CHAPTER 7

Evidence-Based and Evidence-Informed Programs

In addition to focusing on the content in the curriculum you are teaching, you may also be called upon to be part of choosing intervention or prevention programs to meet social, emotional, or behavioral needs of students.

Your input is important in order for school leaders to identify programs that are a good fit with what is being taught in the classroom and with the particular circumstances and needs of your students.

It's important to realize, however, that most—if not all—of the interventions that are now considered to be based on evidence were not designed with military children in mind. Experimental trials or pilot programs most likely never took into account the unique challenges that children in military families are facing.

For example, your school may have a bullying prevention program that teaches children to accept others who are different because of what they wear, whether they have a disability, or are gay. But military children may be subjected to teasing just because they have a parent who is in the military or because they have moved six or seven times and haven't had the same experiences as their peers.

For a military child, engaging in risky behavior, whether sexual activity or drugs and alcohol, may not be the result of peer pressure. Instead, these actions may increase when his or her parent has left for a deployment or after a parent has returned from war and is having trouble readjusting to family life.

Programs and practices will likely need to be adapted in order to address the needs of the military students in your class. An anti-bullying program can include information on military culture, for example. A tutoring or mentoring program can ask veterans to work with military students who are struggling academically. College access programs should include information on military scholarships and rules regarding in-state tuition eligibility.

FINDING EVIDENCE-BASED PROGRAMS

A variety of sources are available when searching for effective programs. These institutes and agencies have examined the research on various programs and interventions and present it in a searchable format.

- The Center for the Study and Prevention of Violence at the University of Colorado has an Information Clearinghouse as well as a "Blueprints for Violence Prevention" project that identifies "truly outstanding violence and drug prevention programs that meet a high scientific standard of effectiveness." Blueprints features both model and promising programs. The selection criteria are also explained. http://www.colorado.edu/cspv/infohouse/index.html
- The Substance Abuse and Mental Health Services Administration (SAMHSA) is part of the U.S. Department of Health and Human Services. Its National Registry of Evidence-Based Programs and Practices (NREPP) includes hundreds of prevention and intervention programs that have been reviewed and rated by outside researchers. Ratings are explained, but they don't necessarily imply endorsement by SAMHSA. http://www.nrepp. samhsa.gov/Search.aspx
- What Works Clearinghouse is a database from the Institute of Educational Sciences within the U.S. Department of Education. Programs, practices, and policies are organized into the categories of Academic Achievement, Dropout Prevention, Language Development, Math/Science, Personal/Social Development, and Reading/Writing. http://ies.ed.gov/ncee/wwc/ A newer, related site is "Doing What Works," which focuses more on implementing best practices. http://dww.ed.gov/
- The Office of Juvenile Justice and Delinquency Prevention, part of the U.S. Department of Justice, offers a Model Programs Guide designed to assist educators and other youth-serving organizations in finding programs that can make a positive difference. The database includes over 200 programs. http://www.ojjdp.gov/mpg/
- The Child Welfare Information Gateway is part of the U.S. Department of Health and Human Services' Administration for Children and Families. The Gateway lists evidence-based and evidence-informed programs in the area of parent education. http:// www.childwelfare.gov/pubs/issue_briefs/parented/programs.cfm
- The "What Works" section of the Child Trends website features the Lifecourse Interventions to Nurture Kids Successfully (LINKS) Database, which includes programs that work–or don't–to enhance children's development. Also in the "What Works" section is a link

to "Interventions that Work." http://www.childtrends.org/_catdisp_ page.cfm?LID=CD56B3D7-2F05-4F8E-BCC99B05A4CAEA04

- A staff at the RAND Corporation maintains the Promising Practices Network. "Programs that Work" are organized into two categories: Proven and Promising Programs, which have met certain evidence criteria, and Screened Programs, which have not yet received a full review by the network. http://www.promisingpractices.net/default. asp

In Appendix B, we list many of these interventions, websites for more information, and some findings on their effectiveness. Again, while we have tried to provide the most up-to-date website address, you should conduct your own Internet search for the program if the link is incorrect.

PROMISING INTERVENTIONS FOR MILITARY CHILDREN

There is still a lack of research-based programs designed specifically for military children attending public schools. One initiative, however, is aimed at helping families cope with the challenges of deployment and reintegration.

FOCUS, which stands for Families OverComing Under Stress, is based at the University of California, Los Angeles. It is a resiliency-training program for military children and families. Participants learn practical skills to cope with the challenges of deployment and reintegration when the deployed family member comes back home. More specifically, the program teaches:

- emotional regulation
- communication
- problem solving
- goal setting
- managing deployment reminders

FOCUS has also been adapted to serve families with young children, in response to research showing that even infants and toddlers can experience stress and depression. FOCUS for Early Childhood emphasizes the parent-child relationship. The family sessions are used to model and practice learned skills. The three main components of FOCUS for early childhood are psychoeducation, creating a family narrative/time line, and skills training in the areas of emotional regulation, communication, problem solving, and goal setting.

In addition, FOCUS-Combat Injury is currently being researched as part of a randomized control study among U.S. Army soldiers and their families.

The FOCUS-CI study will evaluate the impact of this adapted version of FOCUS for families of combat injured soldiers receiving care in both medical and home settings. The study is taking place at Walter Reed Army Hospital, Brooke Army Medical Center, and Madigan Army Medical Center, and is being funded by Congressional Directed Medical Research Programs.

The original FOCUS program is available at many installations across the country and in Japan. In addition, online training is available. More information can be found at http://www.focusproject.org/.

Two additional programs that can be implemented by teachers were not specifically designed for military children, but have been recommended for use with military children struggling with stress, behavior problems, or other issues that could surface as a result of being part of a military family.

Child Adult Relationship Enhancement (CARE) is an "evidence-informed" intervention that is an adaptation of Parent-Child Interaction Therapy (PCIT). This means that CARE is guided or inspired by findings from research but it has not yet been evaluated for its effectiveness. PCIT is designed for children ages 2 to 12 with behavior problems and a history of traumatic stress, as well as their parents, caregivers, and teachers. The program has been shown to improve caregivers' ability to manage problem behavior, reduce conflict, and increase positive interaction with the child.

CARE focuses on the three skills of Praise, Paraphrase, and Point-out-Behavior to connect children with the caregivers. Parents or caregivers learn to give positive commands and to use "selective ignoring" techniques to encourage better behavior.

CARE training can be useful to those working with children in a wide variety of settings, including child-care centers and schools.

Research on CARE is not yet available, but a body of evidence exists for PCIT. More information on CARE training is available from the Trauma Treatment Training Center at Cincinnati Children's Hospital. http://www.cincinnatichildrens.org/research/div/child-abuse/trauma-center/pcit.htm

Support for Students Exposed to Trauma (SSET): This program was developed by researchers at RAND in collaboration with Marleen Wong, an Assistant Dean in the USC School of Social Work and a co-principal investigator for Building Capacity. It is based on a group intervention called Cognitive Behavioral Intervention for Trauma in Schools (CBITS), which is aimed at relieving symptoms of PTSD, depression, and general anxiety for children exposed to trauma, such as witnessing or being a victim of violence, being abused, or being in a disaster. The program was not originally intended for military children, but can apply to many of the situations they might be facing. Through drawing, talking, and completing outside assignments, children learn a variety of skills, such as how to relax, challenge negative or upsetting thoughts, solve social problems, and process traumatic memories and grief. The program includes ten sessions and typically targets children in grades 6–9, but has been used with children as young as 8.

In a randomized controlled study with children from Los Angeles Unified School District, children in the CBITS program had significantly greater improvement in PTSD and depressive symptoms compared to those on the wait list at a 3-month follow-up. Parents of children in the program also reported significantly improved child functioning compared with children in the wait-list group. The improvements were still seen at a subsequent follow-up at 6 months. Results from another study showed that those in the CBITS intervention group had significantly fewer self-reported symptoms of PTSD and depression than children in a comparison group.

While CBITS is meant to be led by a mental health professional, SSET can be used by teachers and even graduate students. The manual provides lesson plans, materials, and worksheets for use in a group setting. More information is available at http://www.rand.org/pubs/research_briefs/RB9443-1/index1.html

The Building Capacity Project and Consortium

In addition to the publication of this resource guide, *Building Capacity to Create Highly Supportive Military-Connected School Districts* has several other components:

- Master's students in social work, school counseling, and school psychology, receiving special training in working with military-connected schools, are based in the consortium schools. They provide a range of services for the entire school community, but primarily focus on the needs of military students and their families. These services include individual and group consultations with students, staff, and parents, and the dissemination of resources and materials designed to increase knowledge within schools.
- Their role also includes parent support, data collection and interpretation, and after-school programs. Their work in the schools is designed to create a military-friendly school climate that can be sustained once the project ends. Schools will be matched with evidence-based programs appropriate for their student population as well as community-based and district-level resources that meet the needs of their families. Over the 4-year grant period, interns will provide an estimated 72,000 contact hours in schools and the community.
- Conducted since 1985, the *California Health Kids Survey* collects detailed information on school climate, risky behaviors, resiliency, and protective factors both in school and at home. The survey is administered by WestEd, an education research, development, and service agency. Because every school district in California is required to conduct the survey, it is a valuable tool for monitoring students' needs and behaviors. The Building Capacity project trains the interns, teachers, parent organizations, and principals to make better use of this data system in their decisions about programs and services for students.

- In addition, the state of California and WestEd have partnered with the consortium to administer a newly created *Military Module* of the survey, which is now available to all schools in the state and nation. This module is allowing schools to examine how deployment and multiple school changes, as well as school, home, and community supports, impact students' social and academic outcomes.
- Building Capacity is also identifying innovative and successful practices within schools that create more supportive environments for military families. These programs and best practices are being evaluated to determine whether they can be replicated in other schools. These ideas will be collected and housed at USC as part of a clearinghouse. In addition, since there are currently no existing evidence-based models designed specifically for military-connected schools, this project will adapt existing programs for use with these students and families and evaluate their effectiveness.
- To build awareness and encourage the exchange of ideas surrounding military-connected schools, Building Capacity is arranging conferences and workshops for administrators and educators in the consortium schools. This aspect of the project builds on the work already started by DoDEA, military school liaison officers, and nonprofit organizations such as the Military Child Education Coalition. In addition, these gatherings will be adapted to address the individual needs of schools.
- Finally, it is our hope that the schools and districts participating in this project will continue this work once the grant expires. Another goal of Building Capacity is that the work implemented in the San Diego-area districts can be replicated in military-connected schools across the country.

The school districts involved in the project are located in San Diego and Riverside counties in California. San Diego County is home to Camp Pendleton Marine Corps Base, Naval Base Coronado, Marine Corps Air Station Miramar, Naval Base Point Loma, and the Space and Naval Warfare Systems Command's Systems Center Pacific.

The eight school districts in the consortium are:

- **Bonsall Union School District**: Located north of San Diego, this is the smallest district in the consortium with 1,881 students. Approximately 9% of the elementary district's students are from military families. The district is 52% White, 34% Hispanic, 6% Asian, and 2% African American.
- **Chula Vista Elementary School District**: Located south of San Diego near the border with Mexico, the 27,460-student district

serves 2,600 military students—9.5% of its enrollment. The district is over 65% Hispanic, 12% White, almost 13% Asian, and 4% African American.

- **Escondido Union Elementary School District**: Northeast of San Diego, this 19,300-student district serves 1,931 students from military families—10% of its enrollment. The district is 65% Hispanic, 25% White, 5% Asian, and 3% African American.
- **Escondido Union High School District**: 9% of the enrollment in this 9,350-student district is from military families. This district is 55% Hispanic, 35% White, 5% Asian, and 3% African American.
- **Fallbrook Union Elementary School District**: With two schools located on the Camp Pendleton base, this elementary district serves 1,500 military students—over 27% of its 5,600-student enrollment. This district is 49% Hispanic, 39% White, 5% African American, and 3% Asian.
- **Fallbrook Union High School District**: Located in North San Diego County, this 3,100-student district serves 313 military students—10% of its enrollment. The district is 47% Hispanic, 41% White, 3% Asian, and 2% African American.
- **Oceanside Unified School District**: Located north of San Diego, this 21,500-student district serves the second largest percentage of military students—about 19%, or 3,858 students. The K–12 district is 53% Hispanic, 29% White, 8% Asian, and 8% African American.
- **Temecula Valley Unified School District**: Northeast of San Diego, this K–12 district is the largest in the consortium with 28,780 students—2%, or 579 of which are from military families. This district is 50% White, 20% Hispanic, 10% Asian, and 4% African-American. 14% of students are identified as multiracial or gave no response.

Evidence-Based Programs That Could Be Adapted for Military-Connected Schools

Midwestern Prevention Project (now called Project STAR)

http://www.colorado.edu/cspv/blueprints/modelprograms/MPP.html
http://www.childtrends.org/Lifecourse/programs/MidwesternPreventionProject.
 htm

- *Goals:* To help youth see the tremendous social pressure to use drugs and find ways for them to avoid their use and those situations through the help of school, parents, the community, and the media.
- *Target Outcomes:* The reduction of adolescent drug use and the involvement of parents and community. [In this Appendix, "Goals" are the overall goals of the program, while the "Target Outcomes" are what is being measured by an evaluation or study.]
- *Populations:* From early adolescence through middle and late adolescence. Programs begin in 6th and 7th grade.
  - ➤ 1,000 middle school students
  - ➤ 20 teachers
  - ➤ 12 parents
  - ➤ 3–4 principals
  - ➤ 4 student leaders
- *Problem:* Adolescent drug use and community involvement.
- *Intervention:*
  - ➤ Mass media programs
  - ➤ School program and frequent boosters
    - ✓ Role playing models in class
    - ✓ Discussion groups with student and teachers
    - ✓ Homework assignments to involve parents
  - ➤ Parent educational organization
    - ✓ Parent-principal committee
  - ➤ Community organization and training sessions

- ➢ Local policy changes:
  - ✓ Alcohol
  - ✓ Drugs
  - ✓ Tobacco
- ➢ Parent-principal committee that meets to review policy and parent-child communication training
- ➢ All programs deliver a constant anti-drug message via all of the components
- • *Resources needed:*
  - ➢ $175,000 minimum over a 3-year period
    - ✓ Costs of teacher, parent, and community leader training
    - ✓ Curriculum materials for school-based program
    - ✓ $4,000 for each group trained
    - ✓ $100–125 for each trainer manual
    - ✓ $7 for each student workbook
- • *Results:*
  - ➢ 40% reduction in daily smoking
  - ➢ Similar reductions in marijuana use and alcohol use through grade 12
  - ➢ Prevention shown through age 23
  - ➢ Increased parent-child communication
  - ➢ The program also led to more development of prevention programs, activities, and services among the community
- • *Assessment:* Regular meetings to assess programs and to improve them

Big Brothers Big Sisters of America

http://www.colorado.edu/cspv/blueprints/modelprograms/BBBS.html
http://www.bbbs.org/site/c.diJKKYPLJvH/b.1539751/k.BDB6/Home.htm

- • *Goals:* To provide adult support and friendship to youth in one-to-one relationships.
- • *Target Outcomes:* To build relationships between youths from single-parent homes and adult volunteers.
- • *Populations:* Youths from age 6–18 from single-parent homes. Also involves adult volunteers and parental involvement for meetings and updates.
- • *Problem:* This program is designed to address the problem of youth violence and drug abuse in the hopes that a one-on-one relationship with an adult will deter youths from engaging in these behaviors.
- • *Intervention:* The program has several procedures that all involved in the program must go through.
  - ➢ An orientation with the program is required for all the volunteers.
  - ➢ Volunteers must be screened by an application, background check, and an assessment of whether they will be able to honor their time commitments.
  - ➢ The youth in the program are assessed by a written application, interviews with them and their parents, and assessment of their home life. This is to help

make the best match between child and volunteer and to involve the parents
and obtain their permission.

> The matches are made according to the needs of the child, the abilities of the
volunteer, and program and preferences of the parent.
> Contact between parent, volunteer, and child is made within 2 weeks of match,
then monthly telephone contact with the parent/child and volunteer throughout
the first year and quarterly contact with all during the entire match.
> Program can last from age 6 to age 18, starting at any age in between. It lasts
as long as everyone is committed and involved.

• *Results:* These numbers are in comparison to youths who did not participate in
the program.

> 46% less likely to initiate drug use during the study period
> 27% less likely to initiate alcohol use
> 33% less likely to hit someone
> Improvement in academic behavior, attitudes, and performance
> More likely to have higher quality relationships with their parents or
guardians
> More likely to have higher quality relationships with their peers at the end of
the study
✓ These figures were the result of a study done in 1992 and 1993 with
1,000 10–16-year-olds from eight agencies around the country. Half were
matched with volunteers and the other half were put on a program waitlist.
The activities of the two groups were then monitored for 18 months and
compared to one another.

Functional Family Therapy

http://www.colorado.edu/cspv/blueprints/modelprograms/FFT.html
http://www.ncjrs.gov/pdffiles1/ojjdp/184743.pdf

• *Goals:* Targets kids who have demonstrated a range of maladaptive and
behavioral problems.
• *Target Outcomes:* To prevent and treat youth with these problematic behaviors and
provide a resource for their families and community.
• *Populations:* Youth aged 11–18 at risk for delinquency and other behavioral
problems. Also involves the parents and therapy teams.
• *Problem:* Youth violence, substance abuse, delinquency, oppositional defiant
disorder, or disruptive behavior disorder.
• *Intervention:*
> 8–12 hours of time
> 1–2-person teams in:
✓ house of participant
✓ clinic
✓ juvenile court

> *Presented by:*
>   ✓ para-professionals under supervision
>   ✓ trained probation officers
>   ✓ mental health technicians
>   ✓ degreed mental health professionals
> Program phases
>   ✓ Engagement which is designed to prevent early program dropout
>   ✓ Motivation which creates lasting emotional changes in the areas of beliefs, trust, hopes, and increased alliances
>   ✓ Assessment of relationships between the individuals, families, and community members
>   ✓ Behavior change which involves communications training, specific tasks, technical aids, basic parenting skills, contracting, and response-cost techniques
>   ✓ Generalization in which family case management is guided by individualized family functional needs as to their environment, community, and resources

- *Resources:* 90-day costs for two ongoing programs are between $1,350 and $3,760 for an average of 12 home visits per family.
- *Results:*
  > Effective treatment of adolescents with multiple mental problems
  > Interrupting matriculation of these students into higher cost programs
  > Preventing younger children from entering infrastructure of care
  > Preventing young adults from entering adult criminal system
  > Effectively transferring treatment effects across treatment systems

Life Skills Training

http://www.colorado.edu/cspv/blueprints/modelprograms/LST.html
http://www.lifeskillstraining.com/
http://nrepp.samhsa.gov/ViewIntervention.aspx?id=109

- *Goals:* Intervention in middle schools to combat early drug and alcohol use.
- *Target Outcomes:* A reduction in the number of younger students doing drugs and a reduction in the number who do drugs in the future.
- *Populations:* Middle school students in grades 6 and 7. Administered by teachers, health professionals, and peer leaders.
- *Problem:* Program addresses the problem of adolescent drug use by attacking this problem early.
- *Intervention:*
  > General self-management skills
    ✓ Social skills on and skills relating to drug use
  > Skill are taught by:
    ✓ instruction

✓ demonstration
✓ feedback
✓ reinforcement
✓ practice
➤ Used in schools for 3 years
- *Resources:*
  ➤ $7 a year per student for curriculum materials
  ➤ $2,000 per day of training for 1 or 2 days
- *Results:*
  ✓ Reduced tobacco use, marijuana, and alcohol by 50%–75%
  ➤ Follow up after 6 years also showed that the program:
  ✓ Reduced the use of multiple drugs by 66%
  ✓ Reduced the smoking of one pack of cigarettes per day by 25%
  ✓ Decreased use of inhalants, narcotics, and hallucinogens

Multisystemic Therapy (MST)

http://www.colorado.edu/cspv/blueprints/modelprograms/MST.html
http://www.mstservices.com/
http://nrepp.samhsa.gov/ViewIntervention.aspx?id=26

- *Goals:* To address the multiple factors in adolescents' lives that lead to serious antisocial behavior in juvenile offenders. This means not only working with the adolescents, but also working with their families and communities in order to address the larger problems that lead to this sort of behavior.
- *Target Outcomes:* To create behavioral changes in the juvenile offender and change their environment.
- *Populations:* Adolescents from 12–17 who are chronic, violent, or substance abusing juvenile offenders, who are also at a high risk of out-of-home placements. The program also involves parents, community members, case workers, and therapists.
- *Problem:* Serious adolescent behavioral problems, such as drug use, violence, and criminal activity.
- *Intervention:*
  ➤ Home-based model of delivery
    ✓ parents are given the skills to deal with their kids' issues at home
    ✓ developmentally appropriate demands are put on child and family by case workers
    ✓ family therapy and strategic planning with a therapist
    ✓ 60 hours of therapy over a period of 4 months, or catered to the needs and availability of the family
- *Resources:* $4,500 per youth.
- *Results:*
  ➤ Reduction of 20–70% in rate of re-arrests

> ➤ Reduction of 47–64% in out-of-home placements
> ➤ Extensive improvement in family functioning
> ➤ Decreased mental health problems for serious juvenile offenders

Nurse Family Partnership

http://www.colorado.edu/cspv/blueprints/modelprograms/NFP.html
http://www.nursefamilypartnership.org/
http://nrepp.samhsa.gov/ViewIntervention.aspx?id=88

- *Goals:* To provide knowledge and help to pregnant mothers in order to create the best environment for them and their babies.
- *Target Outcomes:* To decrease violence, substance abuse, and arrests of both the mother and the child in the future.
- *Problem:* Low-income pregnant mothers are ill-prepared to deal with their pregnancy and the birth of their child and need to be educated and helped in order to be good mothers and raise productive and non-aggressive children.
- *Intervention:*
  - ➤ A nurse visits the woman during pregnancy and afterward
    - ✓ to improve outcome of pregnancy and prenatal health
    - ✓ to improve care given to infants and toddlers
    - ✓ to improve woman's developing career, education, and future pregnancies
    - ✓ one nurse is assigned to a family for duration of visits
- *Resources:* Program costs $3,200 per year for the first few years of the program, later it will only cost $2,800 after the nurses and administrators have all been trained and the program begins to work smoothly. Funding can often be found in government programs for welfare reform, child abuse prevention, and other related areas.
- *Results:*
  - ✓ 79% fewer reports of child abuse by women in program
  - ✓ 31% fewer subsequent births
  - ✓ An average of 2 years or more between birth of first and second child
  - ✓ 30 months fewer government aid to families
  - ✓ 44% fewer maternal behavior problems related to alcohol
  - ✓ 69% fewer maternal arrests
  - ➤ 15 years later the children of women in the program were found to have
    - ✓ 56% fewer arrests of 15-year-olds and less alcohol consumption
    - ✓ 60% fewer episodes of 15-year-olds running away

Multidimensional Treatment Foster Care (MTFC)

http://www.colorado.edu/cspv/blueprints/modelprograms/MTFC.html
http://www.mtfc.com/

- *Goals:* To provide a positive and supportive family environment for juvenile offenders as an alternative to incarceration and hospitalization. Also for youth to develop good relationships with their foster families and to begin better habits and behaviors.
- *Target Outcomes:* Better-adjusted youth who will not return to violence, crime, or substance abuse and who have better relationships with their families and peers.
- *Populations:* Teens with a history of chronic or severe criminal behavior who are at a high risk of incarceration. Families in the community who agree to take on youths, caseworkers, biological families of youths, and other officers connected to the youths.
- *Problem:* Juvenile offenders need a better way to be rehabilitated than going to prison. This program aims to create a more comprehensive and multifaceted program for these adolescents.
- *Intervention:*
  - ➢ Foster parents are trained to provide a therapeutic environment for teens
    - ✓ parents attend weekly meetings and receive daily phone calls for support
  - ➢ Teens' biological families receive counseling with teens
    - ✓ goal is for teens to return home to their biological families
  - ➢ Coordination
    - ✓ frequent contact is maintained between teens' case workers, families, teachers, parole officers, and other concerned adults
- *Resources:* $2,691 per month per youth for an average stay of 7 months
- *Results:*
  - ➢ Youths spent 60% fewer days incarcerated at 12-month follow up
  - ➢ Fewer subsequent arrests
  - ➢ Running away from program reduced by two-thirds
  - ➢ Less hard drug use in follow-up period
  - ➢ Quicker community placement from more restrictive places like hospitals or detention centers

Olweus Bullying Prevention Program

http://www.colorado.edu/cspv/blueprints/modelprograms/BPP.html
http://www.clemson.edu/olweus/

- *Goals:* To reduce and prevent bullying in schools.
- *Target Outcomes:* Better school environments in which there are very few instances of bullying.
- *Populations:* Students in elementary, middle, and junior high schools, all students participate in the program, but students who are identified as bullies and victims of bullies participate in additional parts of the program.
- *Problem:* Bullying and victimization in schools.
- *Intervention:*
  - ➢ Schoolwide components

- ✓ anonymous questionnaire assesses the nature and prevalence of bullying
- ✓ conference to discuss the problem and possible interventions in the school
- ✓ formation of a bullying prevention coordinating committee
- ✓ increased supervision of students at bullying "hot spots"
  - ➢ Classroom components
    - ✓ rules against bullying and regular class meetings to discuss bullying and student behavior
  - ➢ Individual component
    - ✓ intervention with students identified as bullies or victims
    - ✓ discussions with involved parents
- *Resources:*
  - ➢ Compensation for an onsite coordinator
  - ➢ Approximately $200 per school for questionnaire and computer programs
  - ➢ $65 per teacher to cover classroom materials
  - ➢ Program expenses vary depending on size and number of participating students
- *Results:*
  - ➢ Substantial reductions in both girls and boys reporting bullying
  - ➢ Substantial reduction in students' reports of antisocial behavior, vandalism, fighting, theft, and truancy
  - ➢ Substantial improvements in student reports of classroom atmosphere: more positive classroom relationships, more discipline, and more positive attitudes toward school and homework

Promoting Alternative Thinking Strategies (PATHS)

http://www.colorado.edu/cspv/blueprints/modelprograms/PATHS.html
http://nrepp.samhsa.gov/ViewIntervention.aspx?id=20

- *Goals:* To promote emotional and social competencies and reduce aggressive behavior in students.
- *Target Outcomes:* For children to be able to react in productive and competent ways to changes, schoolwork, social situations, and behavioral issues.
- *Populations:* All elementary age students in regular or special needs classrooms should be initiated upon starting school and program should be continued through 5th grade.
- *Problem:* Childhood aggression and behavioral problems and a lack of knowledge of how to deal with these issues.
- *Intervention:*
  - ➢ Program taught three times a week
    - ✓ provides teachers with curriculum for the prevention of violence and the promotion of self-control and positive peer relations among students
    - ✓ lessons include learning about and identifying feelings
    - ✓ teachers receive 2–3 days of training and have weekly meetings with the program coordinator

- *Resources:*
  - ➤ $15–$45 per student per year
  - ➤ High cost involves an onsite coordinator, and lower involves using current staff
- *Results:*
  - ➤ Improved self-control
  - ➤ Improved understanding and recognition of emotions
  - ➤ Increased ability to tolerate frustration
  - ➤ Use of effective conflict resolution strategies
  - ➤ Increased thinking and planning skills
  - ➤ Decreased anxiety and depression symptoms, behavioral problems
  - ➤ Decreased sadness, depression, and aggression

Incredible Years Series (IYS)

http://www.colorado.edu/cspv/blueprints/modelprograms/IYS.html
http://www.incredibleyears.com/
http://nrepp.samhsa.gov/ViewIntervention.aspx?id=93

- *Goals:* To treat emotional behavior and problems in young children through their parents and teachers and promote emotional competence.
- *Target Outcomes:* Reduction in childhood aggression and the development of skills to deal with emotional and peer-related problems in constructive ways.
- *Populations:* Children ages 2–8 who exhibit behaviors of aggression, defiance, and violence. Program involves the children's parents and teachers.
- *Problem:* Childhood behavioral problems with parents, teachers, and other children.
- *Intervention:*
  - ➤ Training for parents: Programs are to promote children's social competence and prevent behavioral problems through games, praise, incentives, limits, and ways to deal with misbehavior. Other programs deal with effective ways to communicate with one another, anger management, and problem solving. Another program focuses on helping children with school and homework, and developing positive outlooks for both.
  - ➤ Training for teachers: These programs focus on classroom management skills, such as distributing teacher attention, dealing with discipline problems, using praise and incentives, building relationships with students, and creating problem solving methods with students.
  - ➤ Training for children: These programs teach children ways of dealing with emotion, how to be friends, how to see from others' points of view, anger management skills, problem solving skills, school rules, and how to be a good student. These are created for small groups of students who show signs of behavioral problems.
- *Resources:*

> ➤ The Parent Training Programs cost $1,300 for the Basic program, $775 for the Advance program, and $995 for the School program.
> ➤ The Teacher Training Program costs $1,250.
> ➤ The Child Training Program costs $975.

- *Results:*
  > ➤ For six randomized control groups of parents:
  >   - ✓ Parents used more positive commands and praise and reduced the number of negative commands and comments.
  >   - ✓ Parents used more effective limit setting rules than harsh discipline and monitored children more effectively.
  >   - ✓ Parental confidence and family communication and problem solving increased while parental depression decreased.
  >   - ✓ Reduced behavioral problems for children while interacting with parents and better compliance with parents' commands.
  > ➤ For two randomized control groups of teachers:
  >   - ✓ Increased use of praise and positive encouragement and reduced use of punishment and criticism.
  >   - ✓ Increased cooperation of students with teachers, positive interaction with peers, and more positive views of and engagement with school and studies.
  >   - ✓ Reduction in conflict and aggression among students in the classroom.
  > ➤ For two randomized child training groups:
  >   - ✓ Increase in children's problem solving abilities and better conflict management skills with other students.
  >   - ✓ Reductions in conduct problems in the classroom and at home.

Project Towards No Drug Abuse (Project TND)

http://www.colorado.edu/cspv/blueprints/modelprograms/TND.html
http://www.promoteprevent.org/publications/ebi-factsheets/
    project-towards-no-drug-abuse-project-tnd
http://tnd.usc.edu/

- *Goals:* To prevent and reduce drug abuse in adolescents.
- *Target Outcomes:* Lower use of hard drugs, marijuana, alcohol, and cigarettes in 14–19-year-olds.
- *Populations:* 14–19-year-olds in all types of high schools using the regular program and experimental ones.
- *Problem:* Adolescent drug use and victimization.
- *Intervention:*
  > ➤ There are 12 in-class interactive sessions which cover a variety of topics that involve the use of drugs and alcohol:
  >   - ✓ Active listening
  >   - ✓ Stereotyping
  >   - ✓ Myths and denials

✓ Chemical dependency
✓ "Talk Show"
✓ Marijuana panel
✓ Tobacco use cessation
✓ Stress, health, and goals
✓ Self-control
✓ Positive and negative thought and behavior loops
✓ Perspectives
✓ Decisionmaking and commitment

➢ Each lesson lasts approximately 40–50 minutes and is for use over a 4-week period.
➢ The lessons involve information on the social and health implications of substance use and abuse, communication and stress management techniques, and self-control behaviors for older teens.

- *Resources:*
  ➢ $70 per teacher's manual
  ➢ $50 for 5 student workbooks
  ➢ $2,500 for a 2-day training program and trainers' travel
- *Results:*
  ➢ For 3,000 youths from 42 schools across three trials after the 1-year follow up:
    ✓ 27% reduction in 30-day cigarette use
    ✓ 22% reduction in 30-day marijuana use
    ✓ 26% reduction in 30-day hard drug use
    ✓ 9% reduction in 30-day drug use among baseline drinkers
    ✓ 6% reduction in victimization by males

Across Ages

http://nrepp.samhsa.gov/ViewIntervention.aspx?id=138
http://acrossages.org/

- *Goals:* To give children the ability to develop positively and prevent them from engaging in behaviors like drug abuse, violence, or early sexual activity.
- *Target Outcomes:* Reduce children's use of substances and increase their social skills and parental involvement.
- *Populations:* Children ages 9–13 who live in communities with few positive free time activities and role models. They may be placed with outside families due to their own parents' inability to care for them.
- *Problem:* Drug abuse, poor social skills, and lack of parental and family involvement in the lives of children.
- *Intervention:*
  ➢ Can be used as an in-school program or as an after-school program. In-school activities can take place in the classroom, after-school activities can take place in a school, community center, or a faith-based institution.

> Older adults (55+) must be involved as mentors. They must be recruited, trained, and spend a minimum of 2 hours a week in one-on-one contact with children.
> Youths must spend 1–2 hours a week performing community service.
> This program uses the Social Problem Solving module of the Social Competence Promotion Program for Young Adolescents which involves 26 weekly lessons of 45 minutes each on social competence training.
> Youth also engage in monthly weekend activities for them and their family members and mentors.
> Materials are available in Spanish and English.

- *Duration:* 1–3 years
  > 12 months of successful programming
  > Mentors spend a minimum of 2 hours per week with youths
  > Youth spend 1–2 hours per week doing community service
  > Twenty-six 45-minute lessons in Social Competence Training
  > Family activities once a month on a weekend
- *Resources:*
  > $1,000–$5,000
    ✓ Training
    ✓ Materials
- *Personnel:*
  > One full-time project director
  > One half-time project coordinator
  > One outreach coordinator
  > Support staff (each working 10 hours per week)
  > Mentors
- *Settings:* Rural, urban, or suburban
- *Results:*
  > Decrease in substance abuse
  > Increase in knowledge about and negative attitude toward drug use
  > Increased school attendance and improved grades, decreased suspensions
  > Improved attitudes of youths toward school and their future
  > Improved attitudes toward adults, especially older adults
  > Decrease in school absences

Al's Pals: Kids Making Healthy Choices

http://nrepp.samhsa.gov/ViewIntervention.aspx?id=116
http://www.wingspanworks.com/educational_programs/about_als_pals.php

- *Goals:* To help socialize young children so that they can express their feelings, relate to others, use self-control, resolve problems, make safe choices, and give them an environment in which they can practice these skills.
- *Target Outcomes:* Reduce future use of alcohol, drugs, reduce violent behavior,

antisocial behavior and increase emotional competence.

- *Populations:* Children ages 3–8 who exhibit early violent, antisocial, or sexual behavior.
- *Problem:* Childhood violence, early sexual activity, drug abuse, and antisocial behavior.
- *Intervention:*
  - ➢ 5–24 weeks for the program
  - ➢ Individual:
    - ✓ Life/social skills training
    - ✓ Classroom lessons to address addiction and substance abuse
    - ✓ Social group work in combination with social skills education
  - ➢ Family:
    - ✓ Parent education
  - ➢ Peer:
    - ✓ Classroom and peer activities created to develop expression, communication, positive peer relationships, and independent thinking
  - ➢ School:
    - ✓ Life skills training with student role playing
    - ✓ Changes in teaching approaches and parental involvement
  - ➢ In-/after-school classes:
    - ✓ Teacher delivers 10–15 minute lessons twice a week
    - ✓ Lessons include hand puppets Al and his friends Ty and Keisha and they involve the students in singing, role playing, and modeling positive social behaviors. Teachers then model and reinforce the skills throughout the day.
  - ➢ Booster session:
    - ✓ Nine follow-up lessons are used with 2nd- or 3rd-grade children who were previously involved in the program.
  - ➢ Parent training:
    - ✓ Sessions designed to teach parents how to express their feelings, listen to their children, become involved meaningfully, hold high expectations for their children, learn to solve problems, and enhance their parent-child relationship.
- *Resources:*
  - ➢ Classroom curriculum kit containing the tools for the 46 lessons
  - ➢ $1,000–$5,000 for the program training and materials
- *Settings:* Rural, urban, and suburban
- *Results:*
  - ➢ Significant decreases in negative behaviors in response to personal problems
  - ➢ Significant reduction in problem social behaviors
  - ➢ Participants are 2 to 5 times more likely to increase their use of positive classroom skills in response to problems
  - ➢ Participants are 1.5 to 4 times more likely to actually use their positive

response skills than children who did not participate
- *Reproduction:*
  - ➢ This program had multiple successful program implementations across the United States.

All Stars

http://nrepp.samhsa.gov/ViewIntervention.aspx?id=28
http://www.allstarsprevention.com/

- *Goals:* To prevent early adolescent use of drugs and alcohol and premature sexual activity, and to help students develop meaningful peer relationships and positive lifestyles and character.
- *Target Outcomes:* Reducing early adolescent drug use and negative behavior.
- *Populations:* 11–14 year olds.
- *Problem:* Risky early adolescent behavior that serves as gateway behavior for more and worse risky and negative behavior in the future.
- *Intervention:*
  - ➢ 1–3 year program
  - ➢ Students are involved in three formats which all involve:
    - ✓ Small group activities
    - ✓ Group discussions
    - ✓ Worksheet tasks
    - ✓ Video recording
    - ✓ Games
    - ✓ Art activities
  - ➢ Students also document their voluntary commitment to the program; sometimes they also receive symbolic reminders of their commitments.
  - ➢ Format 1: Teachers:
    - ✓ Thirteen 45-minute core classroom lessons
    - ✓ Eight 45-minute booster classroom lessons
    - ✓ Optional one-on-one meetings with students
    - ✓ Celebration ceremony to conclude the program
  - ➢ Format 2: Specialists:
    - ✓ Designed for use by prevention specialists from the community who visit the school or organization as experts.
    - ✓ The curriculum is the same as for teachers.
  - ➢ Format 3: Community:
    - ✓ This is designed for outside settings like after-school programs, community and faith community programs, recreational programs, and day camps.
    - ✓ The lessons are the same as classroom lessons but also include:
      - ▪ Nine 60-minute group core meeting lesson plans
      - ▪ Seven 60-minute group booster meeting lesson plans
  - ➢ Booster program:

✓ This is scheduled for one year after initial program
- *Resources:* $1,000–$5,000 for training and materials
- *Settings:* Rural, urban, and suburban
- *Results:*
  - ➢ Decrease in substance use and abuse
  - ➢ Delay in the onset of sexual activity
  - ➢ Reduction in perceived pressure to participate in substance use
  - ➢ Reduced parental tolerance of deviance
  - ➢ Reduction in offers and pressure from peers to use substances
  - ➢ Increased identification and exclusion of negative role models
  - ➢ Increased communication with parents and parental monitoring and supervision
  - ➢ Increased commitment to avoid risky behaviors and set a good example for others
  - ➢ Increased participation in community-focused service projects and commitment to being productive citizens
  - ➢ Increased adoption of positive peer group norms that make substance use, violence, and premature sexual activity unacceptable
  - ➢ Increased student-teacher communication and parent involvement in school

Athletes Training and Learning to Avoid Steroids (ATLAS)

http://nrepp.samhsa.gov/ViewIntervention.aspx?id=77
http://www.colorado.edu/cspv/blueprints/promisingprograms/BPP01.html

- *Goals:* To curb male high school athletes' use of steroids, drugs, and alcohol and to promote healthy exercise and practice programs.
- *Intervention:* Program is integrated into team practice sessions and includes:
  - ➢ 7 to 8 50-minute classroom sessions, covering subjects such as risk factors of steroid use, strength training, sports nutrition, and the skills to refuse steroids and other substances. In addition, nutritional recommendations and false claims of over-the-counter supplements are discussed.
  - ➢ 7 to 8 weight room sessions, providing demonstrations of different weight-lifting techniques, while reinforcing other elements of the classroom curriculum
  - ➢ one-evening informational session for parents
- *Settings:* Schools, recreational centers, and other community organizations with adolescent male athletes
- *Results:*
  - ➢ Less likely to actually use steroids at post-test and 1-year follow-up
  - ➢ Less likely to use alcohol and other drugs (marijuana, amphetamines, and narcotics) at the 1-year follow-up
  - ➢ Less likely to have new occurrences of drinking and driving at the 1-year follow-up

> Less likely to intend to use anabolic steroids at post-test
> Greater self-reported ability to refuse drug offers from peers at both time periods
> Greater knowledge of the effect of steroids and alcohol at both time periods
> Heightened perception of coach intolerance to drug use
> Improved nutrition behaviors
> Enhanced strength training self-efficacy
> Greater knowledge of the effects of exercise and sport supplements at post-test and 1-year follow-up
> Greater confidence in athletic abilities at post-test and 1-year follow-up
> Less likely to believe advertisements for sports supplements and positive steroid use images at both time periods, and sport supplement use lower at 1-year follow-up

Brief Strategic Family Therapy

- *Goals:* To form a therapeutic family alliance, identify patterns that allow for or encourage problematic behavior, and change family interactions that are related to these problem behaviors.
- *Target Outcomes:* To improve youth behavior by eliminating drug use and behaviors associated with it and effect family behavior and practice.
- *Populations:* Children and adolescents from ages 6 to 17 years of age and their families.
- *Problem:* Youth behavior problems, substance abuse, family problems, and problems with peers.
- *Personnel:*
  > Part-time or full-time therapists with a master's degree or bachelor's degree and experience with families
  > Administrative staff is also required to provide support to the families at the most important times.
- *Intervention:*
  > 5–24 weeks
  > Can be implemented in a number of places such as community social services offices, mental health clinics, health agencies, and family clinics.
  > 8–12 weekly 1–1.5 hour sessions
  > Delivered in an office or the family's home:
    ✓ Step 1: Create a positive relationship between counselors and each member of the family in order to form a productive alliance.
    ✓ Step 2: Find the family's strengths and weaknesses and put an emphasis on the behaviors that influence the youth's problematic behavior and those that interfere with the parents' ability to correct them.
    ✓ Step 3: Create a strategy of change that utilizes family strengths to fix problematic family relations. The counselor acts as director of the

conversation and stays plan- and problem-focused.

 ✓ Step 4: Implement plans that sustain and reinforce family competence, change the meaning of interactions, and change interpersonal boundaries.
- *Resources:* $10,000+ for training, materials, and expenses of up to 5 therapists
- *Settings:* Rural, urban, suburban
- *Results:*
  - ➤ 75% reduction in marijuana use
  - ➤ 42% reduction in conduct problems
  - ➤ 58% reduction in associating with antisocial peers
  - ➤ Improvements in self-concept and self-control
  - ➤ Improvements in family function
  - ➤ Over 75% of families stayed in the program
  - ➤ Increased family participation in therapy
  - ➤ Reduced youth behavior problems and substance abuse
  - ➤ Increased parental involvement and more positive and effective parenting
  - ➤ Improved family cohesiveness, collaboration, and child's bond to the family
  - ➤ Improved family communications, conflict resolution, and problem-solving skills

Creating Lasting Family Connections

http://nrepp.samhsa.gov/ViewIntervention.aspx?id=82
http://www.strengtheningfamilies.org/html/programs_1999/16_CLFC.html

- *Goals:* To strengthen families, reduce and prevent substance abuse and use, and prevent violent behavior in high risk youth.
- *Target Outcomes:* For parents to become more involved in the lives of their children and thus serve as a protective factor against the early involvement of their children in substance use and abuse.
- *Populations:* Youth ages 9–17, their parents, and communities.
- *Problem:* Early substance use and abuse among pre-adolescents and teens and the behaviors that result from such use.
- *Personnel:*
  - ➤ Eight to ten well-respected members of the community should be brought together to assist in recruitment of families
  - ➤ Four facilitators who can work with up to 30 families
- *Intervention:*
  - ➤ 25–52 weeks
  - ➤ 1–3-month training session
  - ➤ 15–18 program sessions with youth
  - ➤ Individual:
    - ✓ After-school substance education
    - ✓ Life and social skills training
  - ➤ Family:

      ✓ Parent education and parenting skill training
- How to effectively and positively influence their children
- Enhancing parents' skills of dealing with consequences, interventions, substance abuse, and better communication and relationship skills

      ✓ Follow-up services that get families connected to resources

   ➢ Peer:

      ✓ Peer-resistance education

- *Settings:* Rural, urban, and suburban
- *Resources:* $1,000–$5,000 for training and materials
- *Results:*
  - ➢ Improved parental knowledge of and changed beliefs about substance abuse
  - ➢ Increased parental and youth involvement in setting rules about substance use
  - ➢ Increased use of community services by families, especially when problems arise

Early Risers: Skills for Success

http://nrepp.samhsa.gov/ViewIntervention.aspx?id=137

- *Goals:* To target children at high risk for conduct problems early through comprehensive and continuing intervention.
- *Target Outcomes:* Higher academic achievement in participants, better social skills and friend selection, and less aggression in children and better parenting skills.
- *Populations:*
  - ➢ Youth ages 6–12
  - ➢ Parents of participants
- *Problem:* Children at high risk for antisocial and aggressive behavior and substance abuse.
- *Personnel:*
  - ➢ One family advocate for every 25 families
  - ➢ 3–5 day training course needed
- *Intervention:*
  - ➢ Lasts 2–3 school years
  - ➢ Individual:
    - ✓ Life and social skills training
  - ➢ Family:
    - ✓ Home visits
    - ✓ Parent education and parenting training
    - ✓ Family education sessions to improve family interaction
  - ➢ Peer:
    - ✓ Peer resistance education
    - ✓ Reinforcing negative attitudes about sexual permissiveness
  - ➢ School:
    - ✓ Mentoring

   ✓ Tutoring
- ➢ Core component: Part of the program that takes place in school and summer school, and deals with social and parenting skills and parent education.
- ➢ Flex component: Part of the program for family empowerment, preservation, and resource allocation. Parents and children establish goals for the year and are given access to a variety of resources that they can use to help meet those goals.
- *Settings:* Rural and urban
- *Resources:*
  - ➢ $1,200–$2,000 per child
  - ➢ 3–5-day training program costs $5,000
- *Results:*
  - ➢ Improvement in academic achievement
  - ➢ Significant reductions in behavior problems
  - ➢ Improvements in social skills, social adaptability, and leadership following 3 years of the program
  - ➢ After 4 years of the program participants had more leadership skills, better social etiquette, and chose less aggressive friends with more positive friendship qualities.
  - ➢ Parents showed more investment in their children, less personal distress, and improved disciplined techniques with their children.

Families and Schools Together (FAST)

http://nrepp.samhsa.gov/ViewIntervention.aspx?id=30
http://familiesandschools.org/

- *Goals:* To reduce anxiety and aggression and increase social skills and attention spans in children, to increase family functioning, and to reduce substance use.
- *Target Outcomes:* A reduction in family substance use and child aggression, and an increase in school success for the child.
- *Populations:*
  - ➢ Children ages 5–14
  - ➢ Parents/families of children
- *Problem:* Children's behavioral problems and family dysfunction.
- *Personnel:*
  - ➢ Half-time coordinator
  - ➢ School and parent representative
  - ➢ Two community agency representatives
- *Intervention:*
  - ➢ 1–3 years
  - ➢ Families are offered incentives to join such as food, childcare, fun activities, and transportation.
  - ➢ Sessions involve several families and allow for group and for one-on-one

activities between parents and children.
  - ➢ Individual:
    - ✓ After-school substance education
    - ✓ Life and social skills training
  - ➢ Family:
    - ✓ Home visits
    - ✓ Parent education and skills training
  - ➢ Peer:
    - ✓ Alternative and recreational activities
    - ✓ Classroom and peer support groups reinforcing negative attitudes about sexual permissiveness
    - ✓ Peer resistance education
- *Settings:* Rural, urban, suburban
- *Resources:* $5,000–$10,000 for training and staff salaries
- *Results:*
  - ➢ Decreased aggression and family conflict
  - ➢ Decreased social isolation
  - ➢ Decreased anxiety and attention span problems
  - ➢ Increased social skills, improved academic achievement
  - ➢ Improved communication between family members
  - ➢ Increased respect for family authority
  - ➢ 33% of parents self-referred to substance abuse treatment and mental health counseling
  - ➢ 44% of parents returned to pursue adult education
  - ➢ 10% of parents became community leaders
  - ➢ 86% of parents reported ongoing friendships
  - ➢ 80% of parents who attended one meeting completed the 8-week program

Leadership and Resiliency Program

http://www.promisingpractices.net/program.asp?programid=201

- *Goals:* To prevent teenagers' involvement in substance abuse and violence, and to get them involved in their communities and out-of-school activities.
- *Target Outcomes:* To reduce and prevent teenagers' use and abuse of substances and to reduce and prevent violent behavior.
- *Populations:* 14–19-year-olds
- *Problem:* Teenagers' use of substances and violent behavior.
- *Intervention:*
  - ➢ 1–3 years
  - ➢ Individual:
    - ✓ After-school substance use education
    - ✓ Community service
    - ✓ Life and social skills training

- ➢ Peer:
  - ✓ Alternative recreational activities
  - ✓ Peer resistance education
- ➢ School:
  - ✓ Classroom substance education
  - ✓ Classroom-based skills development
  - ✓ Mentoring/tutoring
- ➢ Community:
  - ✓ Establishment of supervised youth recreational and cultural programs
- *Settings:* Rural, urban, suburban
- *Resources:*
  - ➢ $5,000–$10,000 for:
    - ✓ Consultation
    - ✓ Materials
    - ✓ Training
    - ✓ Program supplies
- *Results:*
  - ➢ 65%–70% reduction in negative behavioral incidents
  - ➢ 75% reduction in school suspensions
  - ➢ 47% reduction in juvenile arrests
  - ➢ Average increase of 0.8 in GPA
  - ➢ 60%–70% increase in school attendance
  - ➢ 100% high school graduation rates
  - ➢ Increased sense of school bonding
  - ➢ High percentage of students became employed or began post-secondary education

Multidimensional Family Therapy (MDFT)

http://nrepp.samhsa.gov/ViewIntervention.aspx?id=16
http://www.strengtheningfamilies.org/html/programs_1999/10_MDFT.html

- *Goals:* To reduce conduct disorders and delinquency in order to help substance-abusing adolescents and those at risk of abuse through family therapy.
- *Target Outcomes:* A reduction in substance abuse, more family involvement and support, and a reduction in problem and risky behaviors.
- *Populations:*
  - ➢ Substance-abusing adolescents
  - ➢ Families of substance abusers
  - ➢ Those at risk for substance abuse
- *Problem:* Substance abuse and behavioral problems.
- *Intervention:*
  - ➢ 4–6 months
  - ➢ Individual:

> ✓ Lessons to deal with youth's current difficulties with school, family, the law, and relationships
> ✓ Enhanced motivation
- ➤ Peer:
  > ✓ Youth's peer group is assessed and the youth is helped to see the danger in having friends who are drug users.
- ➤ Family:
  > ✓ Family sessions, parent-only sessions, and youth-only sessions to address everyday events in the family and family relationships and how to improve them
  > ✓ Important past events that are still problematic are addressed
- ➤ Community:
  > ✓ The family is helped to be more aware of the dangers in their community and the resources available to them.
  > ✓ The youth are involved in a service in the community that will interest them and will help them develop the skills that they need to develop healthy behaviors
  > ✓ Therapists help advocate for the youth in their school and help the parents become involved
  > ✓ Therapists work with parents to develop parenting skills and help them get in touch with services that may help them

- *Settings:* Urban, suburban
- *Resources:* $50,000 for budget, material, and training costs
- *Results:*
  - ➤ 41%–66% reduction in substance abuse from beginning of program, gains lasted up to 1 year after program
  - ➤ At 1 year:
    - ✓ 93% of youth reported no substance-related problems
    - ✓ 64%–93% reported abstinence from alcohol and drug use
  - ➤ Decreased delinquent behaviors and affiliation with delinquent peers
  - ➤ Decreased likelihood of being arrested or placed on probation
  - ➤ Decreased family conflict, improved parenting practices
  - ➤ Significant decrease in disruptive school behaviors and absence from school
  - ➤ 43% receive passing grades at high rates

Parenting Wisely (CD-ROM)

http://nrepp.samhsa.gov/ViewIntervention.aspx?id=35
http://www.familyworksinc.com/

- *Goals:* To increase parental communication and disciplinary skills.
- *Target Outcomes:* To improve children's problem behaviors, parents' knowledge, beliefs, and behaviors, and sense of competence.
- *Populations:* Infants–17-year-olds.

- *Problem:* At-risk or exhibiting behavior problems such as substance abuse, delinquency, and dropping out of school.
- *Intervention:* Nine sessions for a total of 2–3 hours. Parents also receive workbooks with program content and exercises to promote skill building.
- *Settings:* Urban, rural, suburban
- *Resources:* $659, plus $6.75–$9 for additional parent workbooks
- *Results:*
  - ➢ Significant improvement on the Eyberg Child Behavior Inventory, compared with children of control group parents. Children also showed a significant decrease in negative behaviors as measured by the Parent Daily Report.

Positive Action

http://nrepp.samhsa.gov/ViewIntervention.aspx?id=78
http://www.positiveaction.net/

- *Goals:* To improve children's academic achievement and their behavior through positive actions and behaviors.
- *Target Outcomes:* A reduction in youth substance use and increase in students' academic achievement and social and emotional competence.
- *Populations:* 5–18-year-olds
- *Problem:* Problem behaviors, substance use, and poor academic achievement.
- *Intervention:*
  - ➢ Up to 12 years
  - ➢ Elementary school:
    - ✓ 140 15-minute lessons taught 4 days a week
  - ➢ Middle school:
    - ✓ 139 lessons taught 4–5 days a week in advisory sessions or homeroom
  - ➢ High school:
    - ✓ Part 1: lessons for positive living
    - ✓ Part 2: a 44-act play in a variety of settings, virtual reality survivor game
    - ✓ Part 3: interactive, hands-on activities and projects
    - ✓ Part 4: peer mentoring, teaching, role playing
  - ➢ Individual:
    - ✓ After-school, peer-led substance education
    - ✓ Life/social skills training
  - ➢ Family:
    - ✓ Parent education and parenting skills training
  - ➢ Peer:
    - ✓ Peer-resistance training
  - ➢ School:
    - ✓ School change programs to improve parent involvement
    - ✓ Improved classroom management or instructional style
    - ✓ Improved student commitment to school community

- ➢ Community:
  - ✓ Multi-agency activities and collaboration
- *Settings:* Rural, urban, and suburban
- *Resources:* $10,000 for training and materials
- *Results:*
  - ➢ 71% fewer incidents of substance use in middle schools with a high proportion of program graduates from elementary school
  - ➢ Southeastern middle schools: 70% fewer incidents of violence, 60% less disruptive and disrespectful behaviors, 52% less property crime, and 75% less absenteeism
  - ➢ Southeastern high schools: 50% fewer incidents of violence, 63% less sexually-related problem behaviors, 28% less disruptive and disrespectful behaviors, 57% fewer incidents of falsifying records, 25% fewer out-of-school suspensions, 30% fewer in-school suspensions, 12% less absenteeism, and 37% lower drop-out rate
  - ➢ Nevada: 85% fewer violent incidents per 100 students and 4.5% lower absenteeism
  - ➢ Southeastern district: 21% fewer violence-related incidents and 8% fewer suspensions from school

Project ACHIEVE

http://nrepp.samhsa.gov/ViewIntervention.aspx?id=70
http://www.projectachieve.info/

- *Goals:* To improve school performance, school safety, attitudes, and parental involvement to reduce student substance abuse and aggressive behavior.
- *Target Outcomes:* Higher performance in social skills, academic achievement, and problem and conflict resolution.
- *Populations:* 3–14-year-olds
- *Problem:* Poor academic achievement, and aggressive and violent behavior.
- *Personnel:* Full-time, paid staff
- *Intervention:*
  - ➢ 3-year program
  - ➢ Individual:
    - ✓ Life and social skills training
  - ➢ Family:
    - ✓ Parent education and parenting skills
    - ✓ Increased communication between parent and child and between parent and teacher
  - ➢ Peer:
    - ✓ Peer resistance education
  - ➢ School:
    - ✓ Classroom substance education

- ✓ Classroom-based skills development
- ✓ Programs to improve parental involvement
- ✓ Improved student participation and school bonding
- ➢ Community:
  - ✓ Multi-agency activities and collaboration
- ➢ Program Steps:
  1. Strategic Planning and Organizational Analysis and Development
  2. Referral Question Consultation Problem-Solving Process
  3. Effective Classroom and School Processes/Staff Development
  4. Instructional Consultation and Curriculum-Based Assessment
  5. Social Skills, Behavioral Consultation, and Behavioral Interventions
  6. Parent Training, Tutoring, and Support
  7. Research, Data Management, and Accountability
- *Settings:* Rural, urban, suburban, tribal reservations
- *Resources:* $5,000–$10,000 for training and materials
- *Results:*
  - ➢ 16% decrease in overall referrals to the principal
  - ➢ 29% decrease in out-of-school suspensions
  - ➢ 47% grade retention
  - ➢ 61% decrease in special education referrals
  - ➢ 26% decrease in school bus discipline referrals
  - ➢ 33% decrease in special education placements
- *Program Benefits:*
  - ➢ Maximize student academic achievement
  - ➢ Create safe and positive school climates
  - ➢ Increase and sustain effective classroom instruction
  - ➢ Increase and sustain strong parent-school involvement
  - ➢ Teaches students social skills and self-management behavior

Project Venture (PV)

http://nrepp.samhsa.gov/ViewIntervention.aspx?id=102
http://niylp.org/projects/Project-Venture-Model-Program-Info.pdf

- *Goals:* To help high-risk youth through classroom-based problem-solving activities, outdoor experiential activities, adventure camps and treks, and community-oriented service learning.
- *Target Outcomes:* Positive self-concept, effective social interaction skills, and community service ethic, internal locus of control, and increased decisionmaking and problem-solving skills.
- *Populations:* High-risk American Indian youth and youth from other ethnic groups.
- *Problem:* Substance abuse and problem behaviors in American Indian youth and youth of other ethnic groups.
- *Intervention:*

> ➤ 25–52 weeks
> ➤ 20 1-hour lessons delivered over the course of the school year
> ➤ Activities:
>   ✓ Team and trust-building exercises, hiking, bicycling, and climbing
> ➤ Individual:
>   ✓ Classroom curricula designed to motivate pro-health decisions
>   ✓ Culturally appropriate activities and curricula incorporating cultural heritage lessons with activities
>   ✓ Life and social skills training
> ➤ School:
>   ✓ Classroom-based skills development, life skills training with role play
> ➤ Peer:
>   ✓ Alternative recreational activities
> ➤ Family:
>   ✓ Parent education
> ➤ Community:
>   ✓ Mentoring and community service and substance education
>   ✓ Multiagency activities and collaboration

- *Settings:* Rural, tribal reservations
- *Resources:* $100,000 for budget, training, materials, and more optional materials
- *Results:*
  - ➤ Decrease in substance use for participants' lifetimes
  - ➤ Reductions in past 30-day alcohol and illegal drug use
  - ➤ Decreased depression
  - ➤ Decreased aggressive behavior
  - ➤ Improved internal locus of control
  - ➤ Increased resiliency
  - ➤ Improved school attendance

Reconnecting Youth:
A Peer Group Approach to Building Life Skills

http://nrepp.samhsa.gov/ViewIntervention.aspx?id=96
http://www.reconnectingyouth.com/ry/

- *Goals:* To prevent behavioral problems and dropping out of high school, and improve youths' emotional competence.
- *Target Outcomes:* Increased school performance, decreased drug involvement, increased attendance, and reduced emotional distress and behavioral problems.
- *Populations:* Students from grades 9–12
- *Intervention:*
  - ➤ 5–24 weeks
  - ➤ One semester of daily 50-minute classes on four topics: self-esteem, decision-making, personal control and interpersonal communication

- Other aspects involved are school bonding activities, parental involvement, and school crisis response
- Individual:
  - ✓ Life and social skills training
- Family:
  - ✓ Family sessions to improve family interactions
- Peer:
  - ✓ Alternative recreational activities
  - ✓ Peer resistance education
- School:
  - ✓ Classroom substance education
  - ✓ Classroom-based skills development
  - ✓ Mentoring and tutoring
- Community:
  - ✓ Multiagency activities and collaboration
- *Settings:* Urban, suburban
- *Resources:* $5,000–$10,000 for training and materials
- *Results:*
  - 54% decrease in hard drug use
  - Curbed progression of alcohol and other drug use
  - Decreased suicidal behaviors
  - Decreased anxiety
  - Decreased depression and hopelessness
  - 48% decrease in anger control problems and aggression
  - 18% improvement in grades in all classes
  - Decreased high school drop out rate

Responding in Peaceful and Positive Ways (RIPP)

http://www.nrepp.samhsa.gov/ViewIntervention.aspx?id=59
http://www.promisingpractices.net/program.asp?programid=238

- *Goals:* To promote nonviolence in schools and give students other ways of dealing with conflict than with fighting, and to reduce the number of violent occurrences in schools.
- *Target Outcomes:* To lower the number of violent incidents in schools and promote nonviolent behavior.
- *Populations:* Middle school and junior high students from grades 6–9.
- *Problem:* Violence in schools.
- *Intervention:*
  - Delivered over 3 years
  - 6th grade: 25 weekly 50-minute lessons as well as peer mediation group
  - 7th and 8th grade: 12 50-minute lessons over the course of the year. More peer mediation.

> Curriculum includes: Team-building activities, social and cognitive problem solving, repetition and mental rehearsal, relaxation techniques, small group work, specific skills for preventing violence, role playing, and peer mediation.
> Individual:
> ✓ Training for expectations of nonviolence and positive behaviors and achievement
> ✓ Development of self-management skills
> Peer:
> ✓ Mediation training and practice
> School:
> ✓ In-class violence prevention lessons

- *Settings:* Rural, urban, suburban
- *Resources:*
  > $1,000–$5,000 for training and materials
  > A 5-day training session is necessary
- *Results:*
  > Decreased frequency of drug abuse
  > Decreased peer pressure to use drugs
  > Decreased violations of disciplinary code for violent behavior
  > Increased peer support for positive behavior
  > Increased use of violence prevention resources
  > Increased student and staff reports of improved quality of life
  > Increased use of peer mediation programs
  > Fewer in-school suspensions

SAFEChildren

http://www.nrepp.samhsa.gov/ViewIntervention.aspx?id=40
http://www.childtrends.org/Lifecourse/programs/SafeChildren.htm

- *Goals:* To help young children make a successful transition to elementary school and create a solid base for the future.
- *Target Outcomes:* Reductions in problem behaviors and a strong school and community for young children in at-risk areas.
- *Populations:*
  > Children ages 5–6
  > Parents
- *Problem:* Young children at risk for future problems.
- *Intervention:*
  > 5–24 weeks
  > 20 weeks of family group sessions lasting 2–2.5 hours
  > Thirty 30-minute tutoring sessions, 2–3 times a week
  > Individual:
  > ✓ Designed to be culturally sensitive

   ✓ Builds social and personal skills
- ➢ Family:
  - ✓ Helps develop bonds among parents in the program
  - ✓ Develops parenting skills
  - ✓ Task-oriented family sessions to improve family/social interaction
- ➢ School:
  - ✓ Helps youths keep skills through booster sessions
  - ✓ Involves parents in school-based approaches
- ➢ Community:
  - ✓ Education to change societal norms and expectations regarding school and academic achievement
- *Setting:* Urban
- *Results:*
  - ➢ Improvements in academic achievement
  - ➢ Reading scores reached the national averages
  - ➢ Parents maintained involvement in child's school life
  - ➢ Parents gained more effective parenting skills
  - ➢ Higher rates of grade-level achievement and school completion
  - ➢ Improved self-regulation in children and social competence in adolescents
  - ➢ Decreased substance abuse in adolescents
  - ➢ Decreased delinquency and violence during adolescence

Strengthening Families Program (SFP)

http://www.nrepp.samhsa.gov/ViewIntervention.aspx?id=44
http://www.colorado.edu/cspv/blueprints/promisingprograms/BPP18.html
http://strengtheningfamiliesprogram.org/

- *Goals:* To improve family relationships, parenting skills, and youths' social and life skills.
- *Target Outcomes:* Stronger families that act as a deterrent for substance use, improved social skills for youth, and improved problem and conflict resolution skills.
- *Populations:*
  - ➢ Youth 6–12 years old
  - ➢ Parents and families of participating youths
- *Problem:* Youth substance use, aggressive and antisocial behavior, and lack of parental involvement.
- *Intervention:*
  - ➢ 14 sessions of 2 hours
    - ✓ First hour focuses on children and parents separately
    - ✓ Second hour brings children and parents together so they can practice the skills they learned
  - ➢ Two booster sessions at 6 and then 12 months

> ➤ 4–14 families at one session
> ➤ Individual:
>   ✓ Life and social skills training
> ➤ Family:
>   ✓ Communication skills
>   ✓ Parent education and parenting skills training
> ➤ Peer:
>   ✓ Peer resistance education
>   ✓ Social skills and communication

- *Settings:* Rural, urban, suburban, tribal reservations
- *Resources:* $5,000–$10,000 for training and materials
- *Results:*
  > ➤ Decreases in family conflict and stress
  > ➤ Decreased child depression and aggression
  > ➤ Decreased substance use among parents and children
  > ➤ Improvements in family environment and parenting skills
  > ➤ Increased pro-social behaviors in children
  > ➤ At 5-year follow up:
  >   ✓ 92% of families still used acquired parenting skills
  >   ✓ 68% still held family meetings

Teaching Students to Be Peacemakers

http://www.nrepp.samhsa.gov/ViewIntervention.aspx?id=64
http://www.childtrends.org/Lifecourse/programs/StudentsPeacemakers.htm

- *Goals:* To teach students constructive ways to deal with conflict and give them conflict resolution skills.
- *Target Outcomes:* Students with skills to prevent conflict and to reduce its negative effects.
- *Populations:*
  > ➤ K–9
  > ➤ Faculty and staff members
- *Problem:* Violence in schools.
- *Intervention:*
  > ➤ Twenty 30-minute lessons:
  >   ✓ Four lessons on the nature of conflict and its potential constructive outcomes
  >   ✓ Eight lessons on how to engage in problem-solving negotiations
  >   ✓ Eight lessons on how to mediate schoolmates' conflicts
  >   ✓ Each lesson has two different student mediators
  > ➤ Individual:
  >   ✓ Classroom curricula designed to motivate pro-health decisions and skills; life skill training and values clarification and antiviolence models

- ➤ School:
  - ✓ Classroom-based skill development; creating supportive school communities
- ➤ Peer:
  - ✓ Two peer mediators are chosen for each lesson, alternating students so each has a turn.
- *Settings:* Rural, urban, suburban
- *Resources:*
  - ➤ $5,000–$10,000
  - ➤ Training: $1,000 a day for 5 days with one trainer
  - ➤ Materials:
    - ✓ Training manual: $32
    - ✓ Student manual: $12
    - ✓ Video: $30
    - ✓ Audio cassette tape: $12
- *Results:*
  - ➤ 62% of program students reached ideal problem-solving constructive solution
  - ➤ 29% of students viewed conflicts positively
  - ➤ 90% of students recalled 100% of negotiation training the next day
  - ➤ 75% of students recalled 100% of training a year after the program
  - ➤ Program students use conflict resolution strategies in non-classroom and non-school settings
  - ➤ Increased academic achievement and long-term retention of academic material
  - ➤ Students resolve conflicts without faculty, reducing classroom problems

Too Good for Violence

http://www.nrepp.samhsa.gov/ViewIntervention.aspx?id=54
http://ies.ed.gov/ncee/wwc/reports/character_education/tgfv/
http://www.mendezfoundation.org/too_good.php

- *Goals:* To improve behavior and minimize aggression in K–12 students.
- *Target Outcomes:* To give students the skills to deal with conflict resolution, anger management, respect and effective communication.
- *Populations:* K–12
- *Problem:* Violence in schools.
- *Intervention:*
  - ➤ Seven 30–60-minute lessons per grade for K–5
  - ➤ Nine 30–45-minute lessons for grades 6–8
  - ➤ Fourteen 60-minute lessons for grades 9–12
  - ➤ Individual:
    - ✓ Life and social skills training
  - ➤ Peer:

- ✓ Peer resistance education
- ✓ Peer norms against violence
- ✓ Peer norms against substance use
- ➢ School:
  - ✓ Classroom-based education
  - ✓ Classroom-based development
- *Settings:* Rural, urban, suburban
- *Resources:* $1,000–$5,000 for budget, training, and material costs
- *Results:*
  - ➢ Improvements in emotional competence
  - ➢ Improvements in social and conflict resolution skills
  - ➢ Improvements in communication skills
  - ➢ More frequent use of personal and social skills
  - ➢ More pro-social behavior
  - ➢ Increase in negative attitude toward drugs and violence
  - ➢ Improved perceived peer norms
  - ➢ Improved peer disapproval of substance use and knowledge of its harm
  - ➢ Improved emotional competency and self-efficacy
  - ➢ Improved goal setting and decisionmaking skills
  - ➢ 45%–58% reduction in substance use

References

Amen, D., Jellen, L., Merves, E., & Lee, R. (1988). Minimizing the impact of deployment separation on military children: Stages, current preventative efforts and system recommendations. *Military Medicine, 153*(9), 441–446.

Baker, A. (2008). *Life in the U.S. armed forces: (Not) just another job.* Westport, CT: Praeger Security International.

Bradshaw, C. P., Sudhinaraset, M., Mmari, K., & Blum, R. (2010). School transitions among military adolescents: A qualitative study of stress and coping. *School Psychology Review, 39*(1), 84–105.

Burkam, D. T., Lee, V. E., & Dwyer, J. (2009, June 29–30). School mobility in the early elementary grades: Frequency and impact from nationally representative data. Prepared for the Workshop on the Impact of Mobility and Change on the Lives of Young Children, Schools, and Neighborhoods, Washington, DC.

Chartrand, M. M., Frank, D. A., White, L. F., & Shope, T. R. (2008). Effect of parents' wartime deployment on the behavior of young children in military families. *Journal of Pediatric Adolescent Medicine, 162*(11), 1009–1014.

Council of State Governments. (2008). Interstate compact on educational opportunity for military children: Legislative resource kit. Available at http://www.csg.org/programs/policyprograms/NCIC/MIC3ResourcesandPublications.aspx

Exum, H. A., Coll, J. E., & Weiss, E. L. (2011). *A civilian primer for counseling military veterans* (2nd ed.). Deer Park, NY: Linus Publications.

Figley, C. R. (1993). Weathering the storm at home: War-related family stress and coping. In F. W. Kaslow (Ed.), *The military family in peace and war* (pp. 163–172). New York: Springer.

Flake, E. M., Davis, B. E., Johnson, P. L., & Middleton, L. S. (2009). The psychosocial effects of deployment on military children. *Journal of Developmental and Behavioral Pediatrics, 30*(4), 271–278.

Goldman, L. (2000). *Life & loss: A guide to help grieving children* (2nd ed.). New York: Routledge.

Gorman, G. H., Eide, M., & Hisle-Gorman, E. (2010). Wartime military deployment and increased pediatric mental health and behavioral complaints. *Pediatrics, 126*(6), 1058–1066.

Grant, L., Stronge, J. H., & Popp, P. (2008). *Effective teaching and at-risk/highly mobile students: What do award-winning teachers do?* Greensboro, NC: National Center for Homeless Education.

Gruman, D. H., Harachi, T. W., Abbott, R. D., Catalano, R. F., & Fleming, C. B. (2008). Longitudinal effects of student mobility on three dimensions of elementary school engagement. *Child Development, 79*(6), 1833–1852.

Kerbow, D., Azcoitia, C., & Buell, B. (2003). Student mobility and local school improvement in Chicago. *The Journal of Negro Education, 72*(1), 158–164.

Little, R. W. (1971). The military family. In R. W. Little (Ed.), *Handbook of military institutions* (pp. 247–270). Beverly Hills, CA: Sage.

Mansfield, A., Kaufman, J., Engel, C., & Gaynes, B. (2011). Deployment and mental health diagnoses among children of U.S. Army personnel. *Archives of Pediatrics and Adolescent Medicine* [advance online publication]. Available at http://archpedi. amaassn.org/cgi/content/abstract/archpediatrics.2011.123v1

O'Brien, A. M. (2007). The effect of mobility on the academic achievement of military dependent children and their civilian peers. Peabody College for Teachers of Vanderbilt University.

Paden, L. B., & Pezor, L. J. (1993). Uniforms and youth: The military child and his or her family. In F. W. Kaslow, *The military family in peace and war* (pp. 3–24). New York: Springer.

Richardson, A., Chandra, A., Martin, L., Setodji, C. M., Hallmark, B. W., Campbell, N. F., Hawkins, S., & Grady, P. (2011). *Effects of soldiers' deployment on children's academic performance and behavioral health.* Santa Monica, CA: RAND.

Segal, M. W. (1989). The nature of work and family linkages: A theoretical perspective. In G. L. Bowen & D. K. Orthner, *The organization family: Work and family linkages in the U.S. military* (pp. 3–36). New York: Praeger.

Smrekar, C. E., & Owens, D. E. (2003). "It's a way of life for us": High mobility and high achievement in Department of Defense schools. *The Journal of Negro Education, 72*(1), 165–177.

Wood, D., Halfon, N., Scarlata, D., Newacheck, P., & Nessim, S. (1993). Impact of family relocation on children's growth, development, school function, and behavior. *Journal of the American Medical Association, 270*(11), 1334–1338.

Index

About the Authors

Ron Avi Astor, Ph.D., is the Richard M. and Ann L. Thor Professor of Urban Social Development at the School of Social Work and Rossier School of Education at the University of Southern California. His past work examined the role of the physical, social-organizational, and cultural contexts in schools related to different kinds of school violence (e.g., sexual harassment, bullying, school fights, emotional abuse, weapon use, teacher/child violence). Most recently, his research has examined supportive school climates in military-connected schools.

Linda Jacobson is the editor and writer for the Building Capacity project in the School of Social Work at the University of Southern California. She is a longtime national education reporter and has specialized in writing about early childhood education, state policy, teaching issues, and education research.

Rami Benbenishty, Ph.D., is a professor at Luis and Gaby Wiesfeld School of Social Work of Bar Ilan University and the head of research and evaluation at Haruv Institute. His past research includes numerous published studies on school violence and children, youth at risk, and the implementation of a large-scale school violence prevention model in Israel. Dr. Benbenishty is also an advocate of children's rights and serves on numerous public committees addressing children's needs and rights.

Hazel R. Atuel, Ph.D., is a research assistant professor and project manager of the Building Capacity Consortium. She is a social psychologist and program evaluator, and has expertise in the areas of health disparities, social identities, stereotyping, prejudice, and discrimination. She has managed several large-scale, federally funded projects, including San Diego Unified School District's Safe Schools/Healthy Students initiative and the San Diego Navy Experiment, funded by the Department of Defense in collaboration with the National Institute of Mental Health.

Tamika Gilreath, Ph.D., is an assistant professor in the School of Social Work at the University of Southern California. She has worked on several projects related to substance use including biomedical studies of smoking patterns and performing secondary data analyses of the correlates of smoking among African American youth and adult samples. Her primary research interests include health disparities and patterns of co-morbidity of substance use, and poor mental health among African American youth.

Marleen Wong, Ph.D., is a clinical professor and assistant dean for Field Education in the University of Southern California, School of Social Work. She has been called the "architect of school safety programs," for her work in developing mental health recovery programs, crisis, and disaster training for school districts and law enforcement in the United States, Canada, Israel, and Asia. Formerly, she served as the director of crisis counseling and intervention services for the Los Angeles Unified School District.

Kris M. Tunac De Pedro, Ed.M., is a Ph.D. candidate at the Rossier School of Education, University of Southern California. His research interests include school climate, data-driven decisionmaking, the use of epidemiological research methods in educational research, and military-connected schools.

Monica Christina Esqueda is a Ph.D. student at the Rossier School of Education at the University of Southern California. Her research interests include emerging student populations, student experiences, and the impact of national-, state-, and local-level policies on student experiences.

Joey Nuñez Estrada Jr., Ph.D., is an assistant professor at the College of Education, San Diego State University. His research interests include school violence, street gang culture, school-based intervention, resiliency, and youth empowerment. His work has been published in major academic journals and he has presented his research at various conferences. He is currently conducting research on the risk and protective factors for gang-involved youth within school communities.